PANETTERIA

PANETTERIA
GENNARO'S ITALIAN BAKERY

GENNARO CONTALDO

PHOTOGRAPHY BY DAN JONES

Interlink Books

An imprint of Interlink Publishing Group, Inc.
Northampton, Massachusetts

CONTENTS

INTRODUCTION

When I first heard that my publisher was interested in doing a book about bread and baking, I was so excited! Baking, especially bread, has always been my passion—in fact, if my career hadn't gone down the route it has, I would have been a baker. Those three simple ingredients—flour, yeast, water—and what they are transformed into has always fascinated me. Even as a young boy, I would spend hours at my uncle's bakery just watching as he mixed, kneaded, pulled, shaped, and baked, pushing and turning loaves in and out of his big wood-fired oven. The smell was irresistible and I couldn't wait to taste whatever *panino* he would let me have. My mother also baked, usually once a week, and on that morning I would awake to that dreamy smell of home baking that made me jump out of bed ravenous and run into the warmth of the smoke-filled kitchen.

When I worked at The Neal Street Restaurant, and later at my own restaurant, I would arrive very early—in fact often during the night—so I could do the day's baking—bread, focaccia, *torte salate*, perhaps pastry for *crostata*, depending on the day's menu, and seasonal bakes like *Pastiera di Grano* at Easter or *Panettoncini* at Christmas. I loved starting my day like this—it was like a ritual—from lighting the ovens, mixing the yeast, watching those bubbles appear, leaving the dough to rise, and that magical moment when the baked goodies came out of the oven.

For me, baking is an almost magical process; it never ceases to amaze me that a few simple ingredients, mixed together and placed in the oven, produce such incredible, mouth-watering delicacies that the world over craves. Take cakes, for instance; that mushy mixture made up in a bowl transforms itself into something wonderful, giving pleasure to many—it may be for a birthday or simply for teatime, but is always a joy.

There is always a kind of excitement when baking, for whatever reason or occasion, an anticipation of how the bread, cake, cookies, focaccia, or pie will turn out, and the smells of home baking are heavenly, filling the house with a warm feeling and irresistible aroma no air freshener can ever match! Whether you bake or not, are an expert or just like to try a recipe from time to time, I think everyone loves the idea of home baking. Young children love to experiment with dough or pastry and make their own shapes, or help mix a cake and then lick the spoon! The taste of any home-baked goods can never be matched by commercially produced products.

Wherever I am in Italy, I always like to check out the local *panetteria* (bakery), or in smaller villages, this is known as *forno* (oven), to see which delicious regional varieties they offer—not only bread but focaccia, *torte salate*, tarts, cookies, and cakes. I never leave empty-handed and love to try their specialties. Local bakeries in Italy bake all of their own goods and have often been family-run for generations, so you know what you are consuming is good-quality home-produced stuff. Some larger *panetterie*, especially in bigger towns and cities, offer drinks and you can sit or stand at the counter to enjoy an espresso and brioche at breakfast or a *pizzetta* for a quick lunch.

Traditionally, the *forno* or *panetteria* was a place for locals to meet up, especially in small towns and villages. Not everyone had an oven at home, so it was quite normal for housewives to make the bread dough and perhaps other baked goods and take them along to the bakery to be baked in the wood-fired oven. Lots of people did this, so a different mark would be made on each loaf so it could be returned to the right person. I remember this was still quite common when I was a little boy and the bakery was always a busy place. The families who owned pieces of land for the purpose of growing their own produce often had an oven built nearby so they could do their baking there as well as work on their land.

Although all of the recipes in this book have been tested in a conventional oven, I love the old wood-fired ovens, so a few years ago, I had one built in my backyard. I love baking bread and pizza in it—the smell and taste transport me back to my childhood.

Bread and baked goods mean tradition. And bakeries honor these traditions when certain breads and goods are made to celebrate the feast day of a local patron saint or during festivities like Christmas, Easter, and *Carnevale*. Each region has its own specialties, which once symbolized a ritual, or perhaps were made for nobility, or even came about as *cucina povera* (poor man's food)—now those specialties are symbols of that tradition and have become part of that town's or region's culture. Quite often a town will be famous for that particular product, and *sagre* (food festivals) are held in honor of it.

I love the history of how a foodstuff has evolved and in Italy there are so many stories, but to include them all would mean writing volumes. So in this book I would like to share a selection of my favorite easy-to-create recipes for products that can be found in a typical Italian bakery—some traditional, some unusual to a particular area, and some with a modern twist.

Enjoy, and happy baking!

FLOURS

FOR MAKING BREAD, PIZZA, FOCACCIA, AND PAN DOLCI

Use good-quality bread flour, which has more protein and is ideal for bread making. I like to use Canadian bread flour, which has a high gluten content, available from good supermarkets.

I also use Italian Manitoba 00 flour, which has a high protein content and is available from good Italian delis and online. This should not to be confused with "00" flour for pasta making. Always check what is written on the package and make sure it is suitable for bread making before using.

Semola di grano duro rimacinata (fine-ground hard durum wheat semolina flour) is good for rustic breads, such as Altamura, giving the bread its classic yellow color. Again, this flour can be found in good Italian delis or online.

FOR PASTRIES AND COOKIES

Use a good-quality all-purpose flour, which is made with softer wheats, and is widely available. I have noticed a lot of brands now specify on their packages what the flour is suitable for, so always check on the label before buying.

FOR CAKES

A good-quality self-rising flour. Alternatively, you can add baking powder to all-purpose or cake flour. In Italy, baking powder is sold in sachets known as *lievito per dolci* (raising agent for cakes). Again, always check the package before using.

GLUTEN-FREE FLOUR

An excellent range of gluten-free flours are now available for bread and other baking purposes, as well as a gluten-free baking powder.

Chickpea, chestnut, rice, potato, polenta, and almond flours are all gluten-free; however, don't just substitute these with regular flours, since whatever you are making may not turn out as well as you wanted it to be. A lot of these flours have to be mixed with other flours to obtain the correct strength and consistency, so always follow the recipes when making gluten-free and check the labels on packages. Recipes that are totally gluten-free are highlighted in this book.

YEAST

Yeast is an organism of the fungus family that is used as a rising agent in breads and other baked goods. For the dough to rise, the yeast needs to grow, and for this it requires a combination of moisture, warmth, and food. Yeast is alive and needs to be treated correctly— that is why lukewarm water or milk is used to dissolve the yeast before it is added to the flour. Yeast typically comes in three forms—fresh, active-dry, and instant.

FRESH YEAST

This is sometimes known as compressed yeast or cake yeast. I like to use fresh yeast and find that it produces the best results. It can be bought from bakeries and supermarkets with an in-store bakery or in the refrigerated section of some grocery stores. I find it such a shame that fresh yeast is not more widely available. In Italy, most supermarkets sell 1oz/25g packaged cubes of fresh yeast in their fridge section, which is perfect for domestic use. Elsewhere, it is usually sold in large blocks so what you don't use, you should wrap very tightly in plastic wrap and store in the refrigerator for up to two weeks. If you freeze fresh yeast, make sure it is tightly wrapped and it will probably keep for up to a month.

ACTIVE-DRY YEAST AND INSTANT YEAST

Despite my preference for fresh, I always keep some active-dry yeast in my pantry. These are fresh yeasts that have been dried and are much more concentrated than the fresh variety. Active-dry yeast is usually sold in jars or ¼oz/7g envelopes and needs to be dissolved in warm liquid, the same way as fresh yeast.

Instant yeast is usually sold in ¼oz/7g envelopes and combined with flour before adding the liquid.

I have used fresh yeast throughout this book, but if you don't have it, then please do use the dried variety, but always check the instructions on the label for quantities before using.

BIGA

A *biga* (starter dough) has been used in Italian bread making since yeast has been around. It helps boost the performance of bread, as well as adding a light, open texture and maintaining the bread for longer. It is made daily with a tiny amount of fresh yeast, water, and the same flour that the bread will be made out of. Extra yeast is also added to speed up rising times; however, bread can be made with just the *biga* as long as it is left to rise for longer. This is my version of an Italian *biga* used to make Puglian Bread (see p.48).

2g fresh yeast (or a pinch/1g active-dry yeast)
⅔ cup/150ml lukewarm water
1 cup/4½oz/120g white bread flour or ¾ cup/4½oz/120g durum
    wheat semolina flour

Dissolve the yeast in the lukewarm water. Put the flour on a clean work surface, add the yeast mixture, and mix until it is well incorporated. Cover with plastic wrap and leave at room temperature for 24 hours before using.

COOKING NOTES

• Making egg wash—Lightly beat 1 egg yolk and 1 tablespoon of milk together in a bowl.

• Preparing pans—All the pans can be greased with either a little oil or softened or melted butter. If the pans need lining, then use parchment paper.

• Resting dough—When resting dough, ideally it should be left in the oven with the light on.

PANE Bread

For me, there is no other foodstuff more satisfying and complete than bread. It has been a staple in most countries of the world for thousands of years. There was a time when people had bread to eat and little else; it is one of the most basic foods of human life.

Italians take bread very seriously—it is present at every meal—from dunking into milky coffee at breakfast, to accompanying all courses during lunch and dinner. And the traditional *merenda* (teatime snack) for children after school has always been *pane, burro, e marmelata* (bread, butter, and jam). If, for any reason, fresh bread is not available, Italians always keep a supply of *grissini, taralli, freselle,* or other hard-baked bread substitutes, just in case.

Bread also forms a vital part of the Italian food culture and is intertwined in many local traditions, rituals, feasts, and religious festivities. Traditionally, festive breads were made on the day the village celebrated its patron saint; volunteers would go from door to door with big baskets filled with votive breads in exchange for an offering. Bread and religion are closely linked and bread is said to be a gift from God. This is probably why leftover bread is never wasted and it is considered bad luck to throw it away, so any leftovers are made into breadcrumbs or used up in other culinary ways. There are even whole museums dedicated to this humble, but important food throughout Italy—in Trapani Sicily, Cosenza, and in Sardinia.

It is said that Italy produces over 1500 types of bread. Every region, town, village, and even bakery has its own specialties, whether it's the way the bread is cooked, left to rise, the type of flour, or the shape of the loaf, the varieties are endless and fascinating. Probably the most famous is the *Pane di Altamura*—bread from the little town in Puglia, which a few years ago made international news when locals fought to close down McDonalds in favor of a bakery. The rustic loaf is made with local hard durum wheat *semola* flour, is a lovely yellow color with a hard crust, and has been made a Denomación de Origen (DOP) protected product. There is also the *Pane di Genzano*, a town outside Rome, whose soft white loaf covered with wheat bran has also been given DOP status.

There is nothing more pleasurable than making your own bread and the aroma of a freshly baked loaf is one of the best. It is so simple to make a standard traditional loaf—flour, yeast, salt, and water—that forms the basis of most breads, including the popular *grissini* (breadsticks), which are so often found on the Italian table for anyone preferring a light and crunchy alternative.

For the next step up, enriched breads, like *casatiello*, which is made in southern Italy at Easter, are made perhaps for a special occasion and packed with lots of other ingredients. Italians are also now experimenting with age-old grains like spelt and buckwheat, and adding seeds to their dough for a healthier approach.

Traditionally, bread is made with a *biga* (starter), which is still used in Italian bakeries. A small amount of dough from the previous day's baking is kept and added to start a new dough. The *biga*, or *la madre* (mother) as it is sometimes referred to, starts with flour and water and is left to ferment naturally for a long time, or sometimes organic plain yogurt or a tiny amount of yeast can be added to speed up the process.

THE STAGES OF BREAD MAKING

MIXING

This is when you combine the basic ingredients—usually flour and salt—then pour in the yeast mixture and remaining liquid. Mix with either a wooden spoon or, as I prefer, by hand, until all the ingredients are well incorporated and form into a dough. All the recipes in this book have been tried and tested; however, you may find you need to add a little more or less liquid—sometimes the weather and humidity play an important factor. If you find you have added all the liquid and it is too much, simply add a little flour.

KNEADING

This is the process of manipulating the dough so the yeast is evenly distributed and the proteins in the flour develop the gluten. Lightly flour a work surface and place the dough on it. Place the heel of your hand on top of the dough and push away from you. Using your fingertips, flip the dough over, pulling the dough back towards you. Continue doing this, alternating hands, for about 10 minutes or as specified in the recipe. To check that a dough has been kneaded for long enough, roll it tightly into a ball and poke it with your finger—if it springs back readily and has a smooth appearance, it is ready. Some enriched doughs, such as brioche, can be very sticky, so these are easier made in a mixing bowl or in a stand mixer with the dough hook attachment.

RISING

This is the stage when the dough is set to rest so that it can expand. Place the ball of dough into a large bowl, cover with either a cloth or plastic wrap, and leave in a warm place. This can be near a source of heat, the linen closet, a warm utility room, or in the oven with just the light on. On a hot day, it can be left anywhere in the kitchen. Follow rising times as stated in the recipes; however, you may find that you need a little shorter or longer. Basically an hour should suffice for basic bread dough, but the general rule is until the dough has doubled in size. Be careful— the dough could also over-rise and collapse. If this happens, knead the dough for a few minutes and leave to rise again. You can make dough in advance, cover it with plastic wrap, and store it in the refrigerator, where it will rise very slowly, and then use it when required.

KNOCKING BACK AND SHAPING

This is when you take the dough and "knock back" all the air bubbles that have been created during rising. If you didn't do this, the dough would eventually collapse. To knock back, you simply knead again but only for a couple of minutes. Sometimes the recipe requires other ingredients and this is the time to knead them in until they are well incorporated.

It is now time to shape the dough, whether it is a whole loaf or individual rolls. To divide the dough into pieces, use a dough cutter. Once the dough has been shaped, place in the prepared baking pan.

PROOFING

Also sometimes called proving or blooming, this is the final rising before the dough is baked. Loosely cover the dough and leave it to rest in a warm place. Proofing time should not take as long as the first rising; however, check the recipe and do not allow it to overproof. The dough should be well risen, feel soft and spongy, and if you prod it with your finger, it should spring back slowly. During this time, preheat the oven.

BAKING

This is when the bread goes into the oven—make sure the oven is hot and at the correct temperature. At the beginning of baking, the dough continues to rise due to the formation of steam and stops when the dough hardens and the yeast dies. Check the baking times of your recipe, but all ovens are different and timings can vary slightly. Basically a loaf of bread is ready when it is golden brown all over and sounds hollow when tapped underneath. If the top has browned too quickly, place some foil over the top or, if possible, turn the bread on its side and continue to bake. Remove from the oven and leave to cool on a wire rack before eating.

This is my version of a basic bread loaf. With just basic ingredients and so simple to make, there is no reason why it can't be made every day.

BASIC BREAD DOUGH

Serves 6

semolina, for sprinkling
just under ½oz/12g fresh yeast (or use approximately
    2 heaped tsp/¼oz/6g active-dry yeast, see p.13)
1½ cups/350ml lukewarm water
generous 4 cups/1lb 2oz/500g white bread flour
1¼ tsp salt

Sprinkle a flat baking tray with semolina.

Dissolve the yeast in the lukewarm water. Combine the flour and salt on a clean work surface, then gradually add the yeast liquid, mixing with your hands until a soft dough forms. Knead the dough for 10 minutes until smooth and elastic. Place the dough in a large bowl, cover with a cloth, and leave to rest in a warm place for 1 hour, or until it has doubled in size.

Knock the dough back down and shape into a round loaf or whichever shape you prefer (see overleaf for shaping ideas—there are many traditional shapes you can try). Place on the prepared baking tray, cover with a cloth, and leave to rise again for 30 minutes.

Meanwhile, preheat the oven to 475°F/240°C.

Bake the bread on the bottom shelf of the oven for 30 minutes. The best way to test if the loaf is ready is to tap it gently on the base; if it sounds hollow, the bread is ready. Remove from the oven and leave to cool.

This bread is delicious eaten on the day it is made. However, if stored correctly, it will keep for a few days and is delicious toasted, used to make bruschetta, or made into breadcrumbs.

Grissini were first made in Turin in the 1600s for the son of a duke who was unable to eat bread. Since then, they have become a firm favorite in the Italian bread basket, especially popular with dieting ladies preferring the lighter, crispier breadstick to a bread roll. In Italy, artisan-produced *grissini* bought from good bakeries can be as long as nearly 3 feet/1m; some have a twisty pattern and some are long and skinny. I like to make my own *grissini*, since they can be kept for longer and make a lovely snack at any time. They are delicious wrapped with slices of prosciutto and served with drinks or as part of an antipasto. This is my version of plain *grissini*—you can also add flavors, see p.26 and p.27.

GRISSINI—PLAIN
Breadsticks

Makes about 24

½oz/15g fresh yeast (or use approximately
　2¼ tsp/¼oz/7g active-dry yeast, see p.13)
scant 1¼ cups/280ml lukewarm water
2 cups/9oz/250g white bread flour
1½ cups/9oz/250g durum wheat semolina flour,
　plus extra for sprinkling
1½ tsp salt
¼ cup/60ml extra virgin olive oil

Dissolve the yeast in the lukewarm water. Combine the flour, semolina, and salt. Pour in the extra virgin olive oil and gradually add the yeast mixture, mixing well to make a dough. Knead the dough for 5 minutes, then cover with a cloth and leave to rest in a warm place for 20 minutes.

On a lightly floured work surface, roll out the dough to a rough square. Lightly brush with a little water and sprinkle with a handful of semolina. Using a pastry cutter or sharp knife, cut out strips about ¾in/2cm wide. Don't worry about the length; they can be different sizes.

Sprinkle some semolina on a baking tray, then place the *grissini* on the tray, gently pulling at either side as you place them down. Space them about ¾in/2cm apart. If you want the *grissini* to have a roundish shape, roll each strip gently with your fingers before placing them on the baking tray. Leave to rest in a warm place for 30 minutes.

Preheat the oven to 475°F/240°C.

Bake the *grissini* in the oven for 10 minutes. Remove from the oven and turn the oven down to 212°F/110°C. Once this temperature is reached, put the *grissini* back in for 40 minutes or until golden brown. Remove from the oven and leave to cool.

The addition of Parmesan makes these very addictive indeed.

GRISSINI AL PARMIGGIANO
Parmesan Breadsticks

Makes about 24

½oz/15g fresh yeast (or use approximately
   2¼ tsp/¼oz/7g active-dry yeast, see p.13)
scant 1¼ cups/280ml lukewarm water
2 cups/9oz/250g white bread flour
1½ cups/9oz/250g durum wheat semolina flour,
   plus extra for sprinkling
1½ tsp salt
generous ¾ cup/3oz/85g grated Parmesan cheese
¼ cup/60ml extra virgin olive oil

Dissolve the yeast in the lukewarm water. Combine the flour, semolina, salt, and grated Parmesan. Pour in the extra virgin olive oil and gradually add the yeast mixture, mixing well to make a dough. Knead for 5 minutes, then cover with a cloth and leave to rest for 20 minutes.

On a lightly floured work surface, roll the dough out to a rough square. Lightly brush with a little water and sprinkle with a handful of semolina. Using a pastry cutter or sharp knife, cut out strips about ¾in/2cm wide. Don't worry about the length; they can be different sizes.

Sprinkle some semolina on a baking tray. Place the *grissini* on the tray gently pulling at either side as you place them down. Space them about ¾in/2cm apart. If you want the *grissini* to have a roundish shape, roll each strip gently with your fingers before placing them on the baking tray. Leave to rest in a warm place for 30 minutes.

Preheat the oven to 475°F/240°C.

Bake the *grissini* in the oven for 10 minutes. Remove from the oven and turn the temperature down to 212°F/110°C. Wait for the oven to reach this temperature, then put the *grissini* back in for 40 minutes or until golden brown. Remove from the oven and leave to cool.

Some chopped mixed herbs are added for an extra kick and color.

GRISSINI ALLE ERBE
Mixed Herb Breadsticks

Makes about 24

½oz/15g fresh yeast (or use approximately
   2¼ tsp/¼oz/7g active-dry yeast, see p.13)
¾ cup/180ml lukewarm water
2 cups/9oz/250g white bread flour
1½ cups/9oz/250g durum wheat semolina flour,
   plus extra for sprinkling
1½ tsp salt
needles of 1 rosemary sprig, finely chopped
handful of thyme leaves, finely chopped
8 sage leaves, finely chopped
¼ cup/60ml extra virgin olive oil

Dissolve the yeast in the lukewarm water. Combine the flour, semolina, salt, and herbs. Pour in the extra virgin olive oil and gradually add the yeast mixture, mixing well to make a dough. Knead for 5 minutes, then cover with a cloth and leave to rest for 20 minutes.

On a lightly floured work surface, roll the dough out to a rough square. Lightly brush with a little water and sprinkle with a handful of semolina. Using a pastry cutter or sharp knife, cut out strips about ¾in/2cm wide. Don't worry about the length; they can be different sizes.

Sprinkle some semolina on a baking tray. Place the *grissini* on the tray, gently pulling at either side as you place them down. Space them about ¾in/2cm apart. If you want the *grissini* to have a roundish shape, roll each strip gently with your fingers before placing them on the baking tray. Leave to rest in a warm place for 30 minutes.

Preheat the oven to 475°F/240°C.

Bake the *grissini* in the oven for 10 minutes. Remove from the oven and turn the oven down to 212°F/110°C. Wait for the oven to reach this temperature, then put the *grissini* back in for 40 minutes or until golden brown. Remove from the oven and leave to cool.

I love experimenting with bread, and the addition of ricotta to the dough gives this bread its light texture. The chopped sage leaves give it a mildly pleasant aroma, but the sage can be omitted if you prefer, or more can be added for a stronger flavor. This bread is delicious sliced and spread with butter or eaten with some cheese as a snack.

TRECCIA CON RICOTTA E SALVIA
Braided Loaf with Ricotta and Sage

Serves 6–8

just under ½oz/12g fresh yeast (or use approximately
  2 heaped tsp/¼oz/6g active-dry yeast, see p.13)
generous ¾ cup/200ml lukewarm water
1½ cups/9oz/250g durum wheat semolina flour,
  plus extra for sprinkling
2 cups/9oz/250g white bread flour
⅔ cup/5¾oz/160g ricotta
2 tsp clear honey
1 tsp salt
10 small sage leaves, finely chopped

Line a large flat baking tray with parchment paper.

Dissolve the yeast in the lukewarm water. Combine the flours on a clean work surface, then make a well in the center and add the ricotta, yeast mixture, honey, salt, and sage. Mix together to make a dough, then knead for 10 minutes. Form the dough into a ball, cover with plastic wrap and leave to rest in a warm place for 1 hour 30 minutes, or until doubled in size.

Divide the dough into 3 equal pieces. Roll out each piece into a long sausage shape just over 1½ feet/50cm long and form these into a braid. Place on the prepared baking tray, cover with a cloth, and leave to rest for a further 1 hour 30 minutes.

Preheat the oven to 425°F/220°C.

Sprinkle a little flour all over the loaf and bake in the oven for 35 minutes.

Remove from the oven, leave to cool, then slice and enjoy.

These lovely, super-soft milk rolls are ideal for children or the elderly, who may find it difficult to chew crusty bread. In Italy, for a treat, the rolls are often filled with Nutella or jam as an after-school snack or at children's parties. The addition of seeds as a topping makes them nice and healthy too. If you prefer, you can omit the seeds, but I love them.

PANINI AL LATTE
Milk Rolls

Makes 12

just under ½oz/12g fresh yeast (or use approximately
  2 heaped tsp/¼oz/6g active-dry yeast, see p.13)
½ tsp sugar
⅔ cup/150ml lukewarm milk
scant 3 cups/12oz/350g white bread flour
½ tsp salt
1 egg, beaten
3½ tbsp/1¾oz/50g butter, softened at
  room temperature
1 egg yolk mixed with a little milk, for brushing
a few sesame seeds, pumpkin seeds, sunflower
  seeds, or seeds of your choice

Line a flat baking tray with parchment paper.

Dissolve the yeast and sugar in the lukewarm milk. Combine the flour and salt, then mix in the egg and butter. Gradually add the yeast mixture, mixing well with your hands, then knead for 10 minutes to make a soft dough. Form into a ball, cover with a cloth, and leave to rest in a warm place for 1½ hours, or until it has doubled in size.

Knead the dough for 2 minutes, then divide it into 12 pieces. Roll each piece with your hands into a sausage, then roll the sausage into a snail shape. Place each roll on the prepared baking tray, cover with a cloth, and leave to rest in a warm place for 30 minutes.

Preheat the oven to 425°F/220°C.

Brush the egg yolk and milk mixture over the rolls and top with seeds of your choice. Bake in the oven for 15–20 minutes until golden.

Remove from the oven, leave to cool, and enjoy!

This bread dates back to ancient Naples, when the official language for the rich was French but for the general population, it was *cafone*, meaning peasant. The name was given to this popular bread eaten by the poorer Neapolitans of that time. It is very simple to prepare, with no kneading required; the dough is left to rest for 24 hours. It was traditionally cooked in a wood oven, but works just as well inside a (Le Creuset-type) cast-iron Dutch oven—make sure it is deep enough; the bread has to have plenty of room to cook inside with the lid on. I love the crackling sound it makes when you take it out of the oven! The texture of the bread is lovely and light inside with a wonderful crust on the outside—it reminds me of how bread used to taste when I was a young boy in Italy.

PANE CAFONE
Neapolitan Peasant Bread

Serves 4

just under ⅛oz/3g fresh yeast (or use approximately ½ tsp/1½g active-dry yeast, see p.13)
1 cup/240ml lukewarm water
3 cups/13oz/375g white bread flour
generous 1 tsp salt

Dissolve the yeast in the lukewarm water. Place 2½ cups/11oz/315g of the flour on a clean work surface, add the yeast mixture, and mix in gently with a spoon. Combine the remaining flour with the salt in a bowl, then add this to the flour and yeast mixture, gently mixing until all the ingredients are well amalgamated (you may need a little more water, so add it very carefully). Cover with plastic wrap and leave to rest in a warm place for 24 hours. After a few hours, small bubbles will appear on the dough; this is perfectly normal.

After 24 hours, place the dough on a lightly floured work surface and gently fold over a couple of times into a ball. Cover with a clean cloth and leave to rest for 2 hours.

After 1 hour, preheat the oven to 475°F/240°C and place an empty cast-iron pot (without the lid) on the bottom shelf of the oven.

When the remaining hour is up, remove the pot from the oven and carefully place the bread inside. Make a couple of incisions on the top of the dough, cover with the lid, and place immediately on the bottom shelf of the oven. Bake for 30 minutes. Remove the lid and continue to bake for 15 minutes.

Remove from the oven, leave in the pot for 10 minutes, then turn out of the pot onto a wire rack and leave to cool completely. Slice and enjoy!

This rich savory bread, also known as *tortano*, is traditionally made around Easter in the Naples area. The ingredients and method have religious connotations; the rising of the dough means new life, the shape symbolizes Christ's crown of thorns, and the eggs are rebirth. There are many variations of this bread and each town, village, and family have their own favorites—what they all have in common is the richness of the ingredients that go into it, making it a meal in itself. I remember, when I lived in Italy, we would often take this bread with us on the traditional Easter Monday picnic and a slice or two was really all you needed. For the cured meats, try to get them in chunks so you can cut them into cubes.

CASATIELLO
Neapolitan Easter Bread

Serves 10

1oz/25g fresh yeast (or use approximately 4½ tsp/
  ½oz/15g active-dry yeast, see p.13)
1¼ cups/300ml lukewarm water
generous 4 cups/1lb 2oz/500g white bread flour
1 tsp salt
1 tsp black pepper
½ cup/1¾oz/50g grated Parmesan cheese
½ cup/1¾oz/50g grated pecorino cheese
scant ½ cup/100ml extra virgin olive oil
1¾oz/50g prosciutto piece, cut into small cubes
1¾oz/50g mortadella piece, cut into small cubes
1¾oz/50g salami piece, cut into small cubes
1¾oz/50g provolone (or mature cheddar) cheese,
  cut into small cubes
5 hard-boiled eggs, 2 cut into quarters and
  3 left whole

Lightly grease a 10½in/26cm ring pan.

Dissolve the yeast in the lukewarm water. Combine the flour, salt, pepper, Parmesan, and pecorino on a clean work surface. Add the olive oil, then gradually add the yeast mixture, mixing well with your hands to form a dough. Knead for 5 minutes, then cover with a cloth and leave to rest in a warm place for 1 hour, or until doubled in size.

On a lightly floured work surface, spread the dough out into a rough rectangular shape. Arrange the cured meats, provolone, and egg quarters all over. Place the 3 whole eggs on one of the longer sides and carefully roll into a large sausage, pressing gently so the filling doesn't

escape. Carefully place into the prepared ring pan, sealing the 2 sides well together. Cover with a cloth and leave to rest in a warm place for 2 hours, or until doubled in size.

Meanwhile, preheat the oven to 400°F/200°C.

Bake the *casatiello* for 1 hour. Remove from the oven, leave to cool, then turn out of the pan and enjoy warm or cold.

It is quite common to go to a bakery in Italy and specifically ask for *Panini all'Olio* (olive oil rolls). Soft and light, these rolls are a pleasure to eat either plain or filled with cured meats or cheese for a lovely lunch or snack. Stored in an airtight container, they will keep for a couple of days.

PANINI ALL'OLIO
Olive Oil Rolls

Makes about 16

⅔oz/18g fresh yeast (or use approximately
   3 tsp/⅓oz/9g active-dry yeast, see p.13)
generous 1 cup/250ml lukewarm water
scant ¼ cup/50ml olive oil
1 egg yolk
1 tsp sugar
generous 4 cups/1lb 2oz/500g white
   bread flour, sifted
2½ tsp salt

Line a large flat baking tray with parchment paper.

Combine the yeast with the lukewarm water and olive oil. Stir in the egg yolk, sugar, and half of the flour. Add the salt, then the remaining flour, and mix well to make a dough. Turn out onto a work surface and knead for about 5 minutes. Place the dough in a large bowl, cover with plastic wrap, and leave to rest in a warm place for 1 hour, or until doubled in size.

Divide the dough into about 16 pieces, each about 1¾oz/50g, then shape into round or long rolls or whatever shape you prefer. Place on the prepared baking tray, cover with a cloth, and leave to rest in a warm place for a further 30 minutes.

Meanwhile, preheat the oven to 425°F/220°C.

Bake the rolls in the oven for about 15 minutes, until golden. Remove from the oven and leave to cool before enjoying.

Spelt is a species of wheat that has been around for thousands of years and was a very important staple in ancient times. As well as its healthy nutritional properties—higher protein content and a good source of fiber—spelt has a delicious nutty flavor which, combined with crunchy walnuts, really comes out in this bread. If you prefer, you can omit the walnuts. This bread is delicious eaten freshly baked with butter or toasted the next day and spread with your favorite jam or honey. *Illustrated overleaf.*

PANE ALLA FARINA DI SPELTA E NOCI
Wholewheat Spelt and Walnut Bread

Serves 6

⅓oz/10g fresh yeast (or use approximately
    1¾ tsp/5g active-dry yeast, see p.13)
½ tsp honey
generous ¾ cup/200ml lukewarm water
scant 2¼ cups/9½oz/270g wholewheat spelt flour
½ tsp salt
⅓ cup/1½oz/40g roughly chopped walnuts

Line a flat baking tray with parchment paper.

Dissolve the yeast and honey in the lukewarm water. Combine the flour and salt, then add the yeast mixture and mix into a dough. It will be quite sticky but don't worry.

Place the dough on a lightly floured work surface and incorporate the walnuts, kneading for 2 minutes. Shape into a ball and place on the prepared baking tray. Using a sharp knife, make an incision the shape of a cross. Cover with a cloth and leave to rest in a warm place for 1 hour, or until doubled in size.

Preheat the oven to 400°F/200°C.

Bake in the oven for 45 minutes. Remove from the oven, leave to cool, then slice.

This is a fun bread to make for Halloween! You can make a larger loaf like this one, or smaller individual ones—after the first rising, divide the dough into smaller pieces and follow the recipe as below. I love the combination of pumpkin, chili, and rosemary, but if you prefer you can omit the chili, especially if making for children. Or, if like me you love chili, you can add more or less depending on the strength of the pepper.

PANE ALLA ZUCCA
Pumpkin Bread

Makes 8 slices

2 tbsp extra virgin olive oil
2 garlic cloves, squashed
    and left whole
½ red chili, finely chopped
needles of 1 rosemary
    sprig, finely chopped
7oz/200g pumpkin or
    butternut squash (peeled
    weight), cut into cubes
1 tsp salt
¼oz/7g fresh yeast (or use
    approximately 1¼ tsp/
    ⅛oz/3½g active-dry
    yeast, see p.13)
⅓ cup/80ml lukewarm
    water
scant 3 cups/12oz/350g
    white bread flour
1 egg
1 tsp honey
egg wash (see p.13)

Line a flat baking tray with parchment paper.

Heat 1 tablespoon of extra virgin olive oil in a large frying pan, add the garlic, chili, and rosemary and sauté over medium heat for a minute or so. Stir in the pumpkin or squash and ½ teaspoon of the salt, then reduce the heat to low, cover with a lid, and cook for about 12–15 minutes until the pumpkin has softened. Remove from the heat, leave to cool, discard the garlic, place the pumpkin on a board, and roughly chop into smaller pieces. Set aside.

Dissolve the yeast in the lukewarm water. Combine the flour, remaining salt, remaining olive oil, the egg, honey, and yeast mixture and mix until everything is well incorporated. Place on a floured work surface, add the pumpkin mixture, and knead for 10 minutes, adding more flour if you find the dough too sticky. Place in a bowl, cover with plastic wrap, and leave to rest in a warm place for 2 hours, or until doubled in size.

Knock back the dough on a floured work surface and form into a round ball-type shape, tying with string to make a pumpkin shape (see photo). Place the dough on the prepared baking tray, brush the top with egg wash, and leave in a warm place to rest for a further 1 hour.

Preheat the oven to 400°F/200°C.

Bake the pumpkin bread in the oven for 30 minutes. Remove from the oven, leave to cool, then tear and share!

Chickpea flour is widely used in Italy when making *farinata*, a type of flatbread sold as street food in Liguria. Combined with gluten-free white flours and yeast, it makes a lovely spongy-textured loaf, and with the addition of mixed seeds it's a very healthy snack to enjoy at any time. It is especially delicious eaten with ham and cheese as a nutritious lunch for anyone on a gluten-free diet. It's also simple and quick to make, since it needs to rise only once.

PANE DI FARINA DI CECI E SEMI
Chickpea and Mixed Seed Bread (Gluten-Free)

Serves 4–6

¾oz/20g fresh yeast (or use approximately
   3½ tsp/⅓oz/10g active-dry yeast, see p.13)
2 tsp sugar
scant 1 cup/215ml lukewarm water
1 large egg
1 tsp white wine vinegar
1 tbsp extra virgin olive oil
scant 1½ cups/6¼oz/180g white gluten-free flour
1 cup/3oz/80g Italian chickpea flour
about ⅓ cup/1½oz/40g mixed seeds, such as
   pumpkin, sunflower, flaxseed, and chia
1 tsp salt

Line a 7½ x 3½in/19 x 9cm loaf pan with parchment paper.

Dissolve the yeast and sugar in the lukewarm water. Separately combine the egg, vinegar, and extra virgin olive oil.

Combine the flours on a clean work surface and add the egg mixture, then the yeast mixture and stir well. Stir in the seeds and salt until it is all well incorporated. Pour into the prepared pan, cover with plastic wrap, and leave to rest in a warm place for 1 hour, or until doubled in size.

Preheat the oven to 400°F/200°C.

Discard the plastic wrap and bake the loaf in the oven for 40 minutes. Leave to cool, before turning out of the pan and slicing.

Taralli are a type of unleavened bread snack originating from Puglia and common all over southern Italy. They date from around the 1400s when they were made by poor people as a bread substitute and have evolved ever since. They are traditionally served by Puglian families when guests visit, with a glass of homemade wine. They are made into little ovals and can be plain or flavored with fennel seeds, as below, or other ingredients like black pepper, chili flakes, herbs, or onion, and they can also be sweet. These bread snacks make a lovely addition to your bread basket or can be served with drinks or simply enjoyed as a snack at any time. They take time and patience to make, but you could get friends and family involved in rolling and making the little ovals; they are well worth it in the end, and they will keep for about a week stored in an airtight container. *Illustrated overleaf.*

TARALLI PUGLIESI
Puglian Bread Snacks

Makes about 70

generous 4 cups/1lb 2oz/500g white bread flour,
    plus extra for flouring
1½ tsp salt
1 tsp fennel seeds (or flavoring of your choice)
½ cup/125ml extra virgin olive oil
generous ¾ cup/200ml white wine

Line large baking trays with parchment paper.

Combine the flour, salt, and fennel seeds (or other flavoring) on a clean work surface. Add the extra virgin olive oil and wine, and mix into a dough. Knead for about 20 minutes. Form into a ball, wrap in plastic wrap, and leave to chill for 30 minutes.

Roll a chunk of the dough into a thick sausage shape, then cut out small pieces weighing about ¼oz/10g each. Keep the rest of the dough wrapped in plastic wrap to prevent it from drying out. Roll out each small piece on a very lightly floured work surface into a thin sausage shape about 4in/10cm in length and seal the ends together to form an oval.

Preheat the oven to 400°F/200°C.

Bring a large saucepan of water to a boil, drop in a few *taralli* at a time, and cook until they rise to the surface. Drain with a slotted spoon and place on a clean dish towel. Leave to dry for 10–15 minutes, then place on the prepared baking trays and bake for 25 minutes until slightly golden.

Remove from the oven, leave to cool, then store in an airtight container.

This savory cheesy bread originating from Le Marche looks exactly like *Panettone* (see p.145) but has a more spongy texture. It is not clear how this bread came about, but it is traditionally eaten at Easter. It is delicious eaten on its own or with a slice of prosciutto.

CRESCIA MARCHIGIANA
Cheesy *Panettone*

Serves 8–10

1oz/25g fresh yeast (or use approximately
   4½ tsp/½oz/15g active-dry yeast, see p.13)
1 tsp sugar
⅔ cup/150ml lukewarm milk
generous 4 cups/1lb 2oz/500g white bread flour
1½ cups/5½oz/150g grated Parmesan cheese
5 eggs, at room temperature
2 tsp salt
1 tsp black pepper
⅔ cup/150ml extra virgin olive oil
3½oz/100g pecorino cheese, cut into small cubes
a pat of butter, melted, plus extra for greasing

Lightly grease a 7in/18cm, 16 cup/4.5 liter *panettone* pan and line with parchment paper.

Dissolve the yeast and sugar in the lukewarm milk.

Combine the flour and grated Parmesan, then gradually add the yeast mixture, mixing well with your hands until it is all well amalgamated. Add the eggs one at a time, mixing well. Season with salt and pepper, then gradually add the extra virgin olive oil and mix well. The dough will be sticky but don't worry (if you prefer, you can use a wooden spoon or spatula). Continue to mix for 10 minutes. Stir in the pecorino and place the mixture into the prepared pan. Brush the top with melted butter and leave to rest in a warm place for 2½ hours, or until the dough has risen to the top of the pan.

Preheat the oven to 400°F/200°C. Place a small ovensafe container of water in one of the corners of the oven.

Bake the *panettone* for 55 minutes. Check by inserting a wooden skewer; if it comes out dry and clean, it is cooked. Remove from the oven, leave to cool slightly, then turn out of the pan, slice, and serve.

When I think of bread from Puglia, huge loaves with a thick crust and yellow straw-colored soft interior come to mind, as well as the traditional stone ovens still very much part of the town of Altamura. Altamura, in the province of Bari, has an age-old tradition of bread making and this bread has, over time, become one of Italy's most renowned breads; it has been given DOP status in the last decade. The bread is made with *semola rimacinata di grano duro* (hard durum wheat semolina) locally grown in the Murgia area, and is still made in the traditional way, using natural leavens and cooked in wood-fired ovens using oak. Apart from its deliciousness, this bread was and still is made in large loaves at least 2¼lb/1kg in weight. They're made to last for up to a couple of weeks, still reminiscent of the days when farmers had bread and little else to eat during the long hours spent laboring in the fields.

It was quite tricky to recreate this bread at home—it could be the water, yeast, humidity, type of oven—but after many attempts, my wife Liz finally came up with this version of *Pane Pugliese*. It might not be the same as the Altamura bread that we eat in Puglia, but it was certainly delicious and the whole loaf disappeared in one evening! You can find the flour in good Italian delis or online. I recommend you make this bread in a stand mixer with the kneading attachment, since it takes quite a long time to knead—if making by hand, you will need to knead for about 40 minutes.

PANE PUGLIESE
Puglian Bread

Serves 6

¼oz/7g fresh yeast (or use approximately 1¼ tsp/
⅛oz/3½g active-dry yeast, see p.13)
scant 1½ cups/315ml lukewarm water
2¾ cups/15oz/450g durum wheat semolina flour
3oz/80g *biga* made with semolina (just under ⅓ of
the recipe on p.13)
1¼ tsp salt

Sprinkle a flat baking tray with flour.

Dissolve the yeast in the lukewarm water. Place the flour in a stand mixer, add the *biga*, switch the machine on at the lowest setting, and mix for a minute or so. With the machine still on, gradually add the yeast mixture and mix for 2 minutes. Add the salt and continue to mix for 20 minutes. Remove the dough from the mixer and place in a bowl, cover with plastic wrap, and leave to rest in a warm place for 2 hours.

Place the dough on a lightly floured work surface and knock back gently with a couple of folds. Shape into a long or round loaf. Make incisions

with a sharp knife, sprinkle some flour all over the dough, then place on the prepared tray and leave to rest in a warm place for 30 minutes.

Meanwhile, preheat the oven to 475°F/240°C.

Bake the bread in the oven for 25 minutes. Remove from the oven and leave to cool before slicing.

This savory version of the sweet Austrian-inspired brioche cake is truly scrumptious. In Naples, where it is commonly eaten, it is traditionally filled with pieces of salami and local cheese. You can fill it with anything you like and I have given you a few ideas. You can stick to one filling or, to make it more interesting, you can fill each ball with something different! Perfect for tearing and sharing and seeing who gets what! It's delicious as a nutritious snack at any time or for putting in lunchboxes. There is also a sweet version on p.148.

DANUBIO SALATO
Savory Brioche

Serves 4–6

just under ¼oz/6g fresh yeast (or approximately
    1 tsp/3g active-dry yeast, see p.13)
½ cup/120ml lukewarm milk
generous 2¼ cups/9¾oz/275g white bread flour
1 tbsp sugar
1 tsp salt
1 egg, beaten
scant ¼ cup/50ml extra virgin olive oil
egg wash (see p.13)
FOR THE FILLING:
mortadella, cheese, salami, grilled vegetables
    preserved in olive oil, pesto, sun-dried tomatoes

Dissolve the yeast in the lukewarm milk. Combine the flour, sugar, and salt on a clean work surface. Add the yeast mixture and mix until it is well amalgamated. Add the egg and extra virgin olive oil and mix together into a soft dough. Knead for about 10 minutes. Cover with plastic wrap and leave to rest in a warm place for 2 hours, or until doubled in size.

Meanwhile, prepare your fillings and line an 8in/20cm round cake pan with parchment paper.

Divide the dough into 15 pieces, about 1oz/25g each. Shape each piece into balls and, using a rolling pin, flatten them into small circles on a lightly floured work surface. Place a little filling of your choice in the center of each circle and close the edges well, rolling between your palms to form small balls. Arrange in the prepared pan, cover with plastic wrap, and rest for a further 1 hour.

Preheat the oven to 350°F/180°C.

Brush egg wash all over the top of the brioche and bake in the oven for 25 minutes until golden brown. Remove from the oven, leave to cool slightly, then tear and share.

This deliciously moist and aromatic tomato loaf is more like a savory cake, hence the absence of yeast and no proofing time. I urge you to use good-quality preserved sun-dried tomatoes—if necessary, buy the dried ones and marinate them yourself with olive oil, garlic, dried oregano, and some chili for a couple of days in a sealed container before using. This loaf makes a wonderful addition to your bread basket or you can eat it on its own as a snack. It also looks very pretty!

PANE AI POMODORI
Tomato Loaf

Serves 4–6

1 cup/4½oz/125g all-purpose flour
1¾ tsp baking powder
scant ½ cup/1½oz/45g grated Parmesan cheese,
    plus extra for sprinkling
1 tsp fennel seeds
3 eggs
3 tbsp/1½oz/40g melted butter, cooled
2 tbsp heavy cream
½ cup/1¾oz/50g sun-dried tomatoes preserved in
    oil (drained weight), finely chopped
salt
½ tsp black pepper
handful of basil leaves
4oz/120g cherry tomatoes, leave the stalks on a few

Preheat the oven to 400°F/200°C and line a 7½ x 3½in/19 x 9cm loaf pan with parchment paper.

Combine the flour, baking powder, grated Parmesan, and fennel seeds and set aside.

Whisk the eggs, melted butter, and cream together in a large bowl until well combined and creamy. Stir in the sun-dried tomatoes. Fold in the flour mixture and mix with a spoon until it is all well incorporated. Stir in a little salt (careful, sun-dried tomatoes can be quite salty) and the black pepper and basil leaves. Pour the mixture into the prepared loaf pan. Push the tomatoes into the mixture (reserving the ones with stalks), sprinkle with a little Parmesan, and place the tomatoes with stalks on top for decoration, pressing them slightly so they stay on.

Cover with foil and bake in the oven for 30 minutes. Remove the foil and bake for a further 10 minutes until golden. Check by inserting a wooden skewer as you would for a cake; if it comes out clean, it is ready. Remove from the oven, leave to cool, then remove from the pan, slice, and serve.

FOCACCIA

Focaccia has age-old roots; it is believed it first came about as an unleavened flatbread, which bakers would rustle up and bake on the bottom of the oven so they could have something nourishing to see them through the long night shift.

The Latin for focaccia is *focacius*, meaning hearth or fireplace. The Romans made a type of focaccia using flour, salt, yeast, extra virgin olive oil, and water, cooking it on the hearth and using it to dip into soup.

Focaccia, as we know it today, originated in the northwestern region of Liguria: the two main varieties are the *fugassa*, sometimes known as *schiacciata*, from Genova—the classic dimpled flatbread with extra virgin olive oil and salt; the other, from the town of Recco, is made with oozing soft cheese in the middle.

Legend tells us that Ligurian focaccia started off as a survival food during the Saracen invasions—people would flee the coast seeking refuge inland and using ingredients they could find to cook with, like flour, water, extra virgin olive oil, and local soft cheese. By combining these few simple ingredients, a type of focaccia was made. This story has eventually led to making the *Focaccia al Formaggio di Recco* a trademark, with strict guidelines on the type of ingredients used and how it should be made for it to be recognized as authentic.

In Liguria, focaccia is a popular street food and stalls selling *fugassa* (as it is called in the local dialect) are many. Locals even eat focaccia for breakfast, dipping it into their cappuccino.

In the rest of Italy, focaccia is often a term loosely applied to all sorts of baked goods, both savory and sweet. I remember, as child growing up in southern Italy, my mom would often ask me to pick up a sweet focaccia from the bakery that was like a cake and nothing to do with an oily flatbread. In other parts too, focaccia can mean totally different things—in Lucania, a pepper bread called *Strazzata* (see p.70) is known as a focaccia. And in Puglia, they make one stuffed and rolled—*Focaccia Arrotolata* (see p.65). In Sicily, a round focaccia is made, topped with a tomato and anchovy sauce known as *Sfincione*.

The focaccia I make is a cross between pizza and bread; I make it thicker than a pizza but with similar toppings. The classic indentations made before rising are so the extra virgin olive oil can penetrate the dough, giving it that oily focaccia taste and texture. Toppings vary from simply salt and herbs to more substantial ingredients like potatoes, onions, or peppers. Like pizza, a focaccia can be topped with almost anything you like. It is often served as a substitute to bread during mealtimes, or it can be filled with cured meats and enjoyed as a snack or for a packed lunch. Leftover focaccia is delicious reheated in the oven the next day.

I first developed this "deep-pan" focaccia recipe many years ago for Antonio Carluccio's restaurant—it was a hit, and I eventually experimented with different toppings. It is lovely sliced open and filled with prosciutto or other cured meats, cheese, or even grilled vegetables for a delicious sandwich. Focaccia is best eaten on the day it is baked, but it will keep for a few days and you can freshen it up in the oven for a few minutes before serving.

FOCACCIA AL SALE
Basic Focaccia with Sea Salt

Serves 6–8

FOR THE DOUGH:
just under ½oz/12g fresh yeast (or use approximately
   2 heaped tsp/¼oz/6g active-dry yeast, see p.13)
1½ cups/350ml lukewarm water
generous 4 cups/1lb 2oz/500g white bread flour
2 tsp salt
semolina or dried breadcrumbs, for sprinkling
FOR THE TOPPING:
1 tbsp extra virgin olive oil, plus extra for drizzling
1 tsp Maldon sea salt
freshly ground black pepper

Dissolve the yeast in the warm water. Place the flour and salt on a clean work surface, add the yeast mixture, and mix to form a soft dough. Lightly flour the work surface and knead well for 5 minutes until smooth and elastic. Cover with a dish towel and rest in a warm place for 20 minutes.

Preheat the oven to 475°F/240°C.

Roll the dough out on a lightly floured work surface to roughly the same shape and size as either a rectangular 14¾ x 11in/37.5 x 28cm baking pan, or a large round pan about 14½in/37cm in diameter (as in the photo). Warm the baking pan in the oven for about 10 seconds, then remove and lightly sprinkle with some semolina or breadcrumbs or line with parchment paper. Place the rolled-out dough in the pan and pour the olive oil in the middle. Using your fingers, spread the olive oil all over the dough. Leave for 5 minutes, then poke the dough all over with your fingers to make indentations. Sprinkle all over with the salt and a little black pepper. Cover with a cloth and leave to rest in a warm place for 45 minutes, or until doubled in size.

Bake for about 20 minutes until evenly golden brown. Check the focaccia occasionally, since domestic ovens often color one side more, so rotate the baking pan accordingly. Once cooked, remove from the oven and drizzle a little olive oil all over. Leave to cool, then cut into squares.

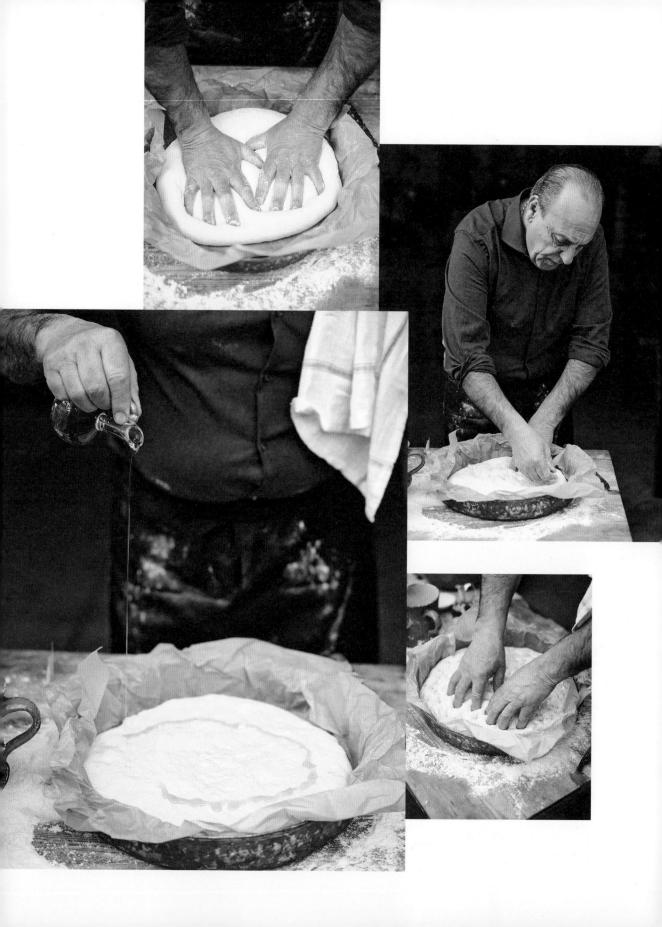

This uses the same method as Basic Focaccia (see p.56) with the addition of garlic and rosemary to give it an extra kick. Like Basic Focaccia, this is ideal to slice and fill as sandwiches or add to your bread basket for a delicious alternative, especially when serving a selection of cured meats as antipasto. I love the way the rosemary gets crispy in the oven!

FOCACCIA CON AGLIO E ROSMARINO
Focaccia with Garlic and Rosemary

Serves 6–8

FOR THE DOUGH:
1 quantity of Basic Focaccia (see p.56)
semolina or breadcrumbs, for sprinkling
FOR THE TOPPING:
1 tbsp extra virgin olive oil, plus extra for drizzling
2 garlic cloves, finely chopped
needles of 2 rosemary spriges, finely chopped
1 tsp Maldon sea salt
freshly ground black pepper

Make the dough according to the recipe on p.56.

Preheat the oven to 475°F/240°C.

On a lightly floured work surface, roll out the dough into a rectangular shape roughly the same size as a 14¾ x 11in/37.5 x 28cm baking tray. Warm the pan in the oven for about 10 seconds, then remove and sprinkle with some semolina or breadcrumbs. Place the rolled-out dough in the tray and pour the extra virgin olive oil in the middle. With your fingers, spread the oil all over the dough. Leave for 5 minutes, then poke the dough all over with your fingers to make indentations. Sprinkle the garlic, rosemary, salt, and a little black pepper over the top. Cover with a cloth and leave to rest in a warm place for 45 minutes, or until doubled in size.

Bake the focaccia in the oven for about 15 minutes until evenly golden brown. Check the focaccia occasionally, since domestic ovens often color one side more, so turn the baking pan around accordingly.

Once cooked, remove from the oven and immediately drizzle a little extra virgin olive oil all over. Leave to cool, then cut into slices or squares.

This delicious cheesy focaccia dates back to the days of the Saracen invasions when people fled the coast to the safety inland, where only basic ingredients like flour, oil, and cheese were available. Hence the birth of this renowned focaccia so popular in the Ligurian region, where it is sold everywhere. The cheese used is normally a local soft cheese, or *stracchino* is popular. My version has Dolcelatte, which gives a more pungent flavor.

FOCACCIA LIGURE AL FORMAGGIO
Ligurian Cheese Focaccia

Serves 6–8

just under ½oz/12g fresh yeast (or use approximately
    2 heaped tsp/¼oz/6g active-dry yeast, see p.13)
generous 1 cup/250ml lukewarm water
generous 4 cups/1lb 2oz/500g white bread flour
1 tsp salt
3 tbsp extra virgin olive oil, plus extra for brushing
9oz/250g Dolcelatte cheese (or other mild blue
    cheese), roughly chopped
freshly ground black pepper

Dissolve the yeast in the lukewarm water. Place the flour and salt on a clean work surface, add the yeast mixture and olive oil, and gradually mix to form a dough. Knead for about 10 minutes until smooth and elastic. Place in a large bowl, cover with plastic wrap, and leave to rest in a warm place for 1 hour, or until doubled in size.

Preheat the oven to 425°F/220°C. Grease a rectangular baking tray, about 13 x 12in/33 x 30cm with a little extra virgin olive oil.

Divide the dough in half. Roll out one piece into a roughly rectangular shape, stretching it by hand until it is ⅛in/3mm thick. Line the prepared baking pan with the dough. Place pieces of cheese all over and sprinkle with salt and pepper.

Roll out the other piece of dough to the same thickness. Place it over the cheese, pressing down well with your fingertips and sealing the edges well so none of the filling can escape. Brush olive oil all over the top and bake in the oven for about 20–25 minutes until golden.

Remove from the oven and leave to rest for a couple of minutes, then slice and enjoy!

This focaccia is made the same way as Basic Focaccia (see p.56), with the addition of peppers and olives as a topping. I love *agrodolce* of peppers—red and yellow peppers cooked in sugar and vinegar to give a slightly sweet and sour flavor. *Agrodolce* of peppers is much better made the day before and stored in the refrigerator overnight so all the flavors can infuse nicely before using it to top the focaccia. Sometimes, when I make lots of *agrodolce*, this is how I use up the leftovers.

FOCACCIA CON AGRODOLCE DI PEPERONI
Focaccia with Peppers

Serves 6–8

1 quantity of Basic Focaccia
(see p.56)
FOR THE TOPPING:
3 tbsp extra virgin olive oil,
plus extra for drizzling
1 red bell pepper, sliced
into thick strips
1 yellow bell pepper, sliced
into thick strips
1 garlic clove, left whole
6 pitted black olives
6 pitted green olives
½ tbsp capers
½ tbsp granulated sugar
2 tbsp white wine vinegar
salt and freshly ground
black pepper
6 basil leaves

First, make the *agrodolce* of peppers. Heat 2 tablespoons of the extra virgin olive oil in a large frying pan, add the peppers, and cook over high-medium heat for 5 minutes, or until the skins are golden brown, stirring from time to time. Add the garlic, olives, and capers, stir in the sugar, add the vinegar, and allow to evaporate, about 1 minute. Reduce the heat slightly and cook over medium heat for about 5 minutes until the peppers are cooked through but not mushy. Season to taste with salt and pepper and stir in the basil leaves. Set aside or, if you are making it the day before, cover and leave to chill until required.

Preheat the oven to 475°F/240°C.

Make the Basic Focaccia dough according to the recipe on p.56, but do not add the salt at the end. Warm the baking pan in the oven for about 10 seconds, then remove and sprinkle with some semolina or breadcrumbs. Place the rolled-out dough in the tray and pour the remaining extra virgin olive oil in the middle. Using your fingers, spread the olive oil all over the dough. Leave for 5 minutes, then poke the dough all over with your fingers to make indentations. Top the focaccia with the pepper mixture. Cover with a cloth and leave to rest in a warm place for 45 minutes.

Bake in the oven for 15–20 minutes until evenly golden. Check it occasionally, since domestic ovens often color one side more, so turn the baking tray around accordingly.

Remove from the oven and immediately drizzle a little extra virgin olive oil all over. Leave to cool, then slice into squares.

The addition of mashed potatoes to focaccia dough is so typical of Puglia. To make it go further, a rich filling of eggs, cured meats, and cheese is often added and the focaccia is rolled up. In this recipe, raw beaten eggs are included and gently cooked while baking. Once cooked and cooled, slices are cut and the end result is like a delicious *panino*, which is a meal in itself. It is ideal to take on picnics or for packed lunches. If wrapped in foil or plastic wrap, it can be kept for a couple of days.

FOCACCIA ARROTOLATA PUGLIESE
Rolled and Filled Pugliese Focaccia

Serves 10

FOR THE DOUGH:
10oz/280g floury potatoes, unpeeled
1oz/25g fresh yeast (or use approximately 4½ tsp/½oz/15g active-dry yeast, see p.13)
generous ¾ cup/200ml lukewarm water
generous 4 cups/1lb 2oz/ 500g white bread flour
1½ tsp salt
extra virgin olive oil, for brushing

FOR THE FILLING:
3 eggs
1 cup/3½oz/100g grated Parmesan cheese
9oz/250g fresh mozzarella, sliced
6oz/170g good-quality Italian sausage meat, roughly chopped
4oz/120g cooked ham (about 5 thin slices)

Line a large flat baking tray with parchment paper.

Cook the whole potatoes until tender, then drain well, return to the pan, and mash. Leave to cool.

Dissolve the yeast in the lukewarm water. Mix the flour and salt together on a clean work surface, add the mashed potato, and gradually add the yeast mixture, mixing well to form a dough. Knead for 10 minutes, then form into a ball. Lightly dust your work surface with flour and place a large clean dish towel on it. Place the dough on top and, using a rolling pin, roll out to a roughly rectangular shape just thicker than ⅛in/4mm. Brush all over with a little olive oil.

Whisk the eggs and Parmesan together in a small bowl, then spread this mixture over the dough, leaving a border of about ¾in/2cm all around. Scatter pieces of mozzarella and sausage meat over the top, then add the slices of ham. Brush lightly with a little more oil.

Roll into a big fat sausage, making sure all the filling is tucked inside and the edges are well sealed. With the help of the dish towel, carefully place the rolled focaccia onto the prepared tray, making sure you place the seam on the bottom. Cover and leave to rest in a warm place for 2 hours, or until doubled in size.

Preheat the oven to 400°F/200°C.

Brush the top of the focaccia with a little olive oil and bake in the oven for 45 minutes. Remove from the oven and leave to cool for 10 minutes before eating.

This is made the same way as Basic Focaccia (p.56), but with the addition of a delicious and substantial topping. The lightly roasted potatoes, pancetta, onion, and sage marry well together to make this focaccia a meal in itself. It is ideal for a packed lunch or a picnic.

FOCACCIA CON PATATE, CIPOLLE ROSSE E PANCETTA

Focaccia with Potato, Red Onion, and Pancetta

Serves 6–8

1 quantity of Basic Focaccia
   (see p.56)
FOR THE TOPPING:
10½oz/300g potatoes,
   peeled and sliced into
   ½in/1cm rounds
salt and freshly ground
   black pepper
2 tbsp extra virgin olive oil,
   plus extra for drizzling
8 sage leaves
1 medium red onion, sliced
2¾oz/75g pancetta, diced
a little semolina or
   dried breadcrumbs,
   for sprinkling

Preheat the oven to 475°F/240°C. Lightly grease a flat baking tray.

Place the potato rounds on the prepared baking tray, sprinkle with some salt and pepper and a little drizzle of extra virgin olive oil, and roast in the oven for about 10 minutes until golden and cooked through. Remove from the oven and set aside.

Heat the 2 tablespoons extra virgin olive oil in a small frying pan, add 2 of the sage leaves and the onion and pancetta, and sauté for 4 minutes, or until soft. Remove from the heat and set aside.

Make the basic focaccia dough according to the recipe on p.56, but do not add salt at the end. After spreading over the extra virgin olive oil and making indentations all over the dough, arrange the potatoes, onions, pancetta, and remaining sage leaves on top. Cover with a dish towel and rest in a warm place for 45 minutes, or until doubled in size.

Preheat the oven to 425°F/220°C.

Bake in the oven for about 20 minutes until evenly golden around the edges. Remove from the oven, immediately drizzle with a little extra virgin olive oil, and leave to cool, then slice into squares.

This Ligurian specialty has age-old roots and legend tells us that it was made for the Genovese admiral, Andrea Doria, hence the name. Because of the border between Liguria and France, this focaccia is also popular in the Provence region, where it is known as *pissaladiere*. Over time, tomatoes have been added to this dish, making it like a *Napoletana* pizza topping, but I like this original version with onion and anchovies. I like to make mine in a square, but you can make it round, rectangular, or any shape you prefer. Cut into slices and serve as part of a meal when you have a crowd or simply enjoy as a snack at any time. It's delicious enjoyed hot or cold. *Illustrated overleaf.*

PISCIALANDREA DI IMPERIA
Onion and Anchovy Focaccia

Serves 6

FOR THE DOUGH:
⅓oz/10g fresh yeast (or use approximately 1¾ tsp/5g active-dry yeast, see p.13)
1¼ cups/300ml lukewarm water
generous 4 cups/1lb 2oz/500g white bread flour
1 tsp salt
4 tsp extra virgin olive oil
all-purpose flour or dried breadcrumbs, for sprinkling
FOR THE TOPPING:
3 tbsp extra virgin olive oil
about 18 anchovy fillets
2 medium red onions, finely chopped
20 pitted black olives
1 tsp dried oregano

Dissolve the yeast in the lukewarm water. Mix the flour and salt together in a large bowl, add the extra virgin olive oil and yeast mixture, and mix to form a dough. Knead the dough for 10 minutes, form into a ball, cover with plastic wrap, and leave to rest for 30 minutes, or until doubled in size.

Divide the dough in half and knead each piece for 2 minutes. Shape into balls, cover with a damp cloth, and leave to rest for a further 30 minutes, or until doubled in size.

Preheat the oven to 475°F/240°C and sprinkle 2 flat square 12 x 12in/30 x 30cm baking trays or 2 x round flat 12in/30cm baking trays with a little flour or dried breadcrumbs.

Meanwhile, prepare the topping. Heat the extra virgin olive oil in a frying pan, add 2 anchovy fillets, and dissolve. Add the onion and cook over low heat for 8–10 minutes, or until softened. Remove and set aside.

Using your fingers, spread one ball of dough into your preferred baking tray. Repeat with the other piece of dough and tray. Top each with the onion mixture, arrange the remaining anchovy fillets and black olives on top, and sprinkle with dried oregano. Bake in the oven for about 20 minutes until the edges are golden.

Although this looks very much like a ring-shaped bread, it is locally known as "focaccia." It can only be found in the rural Lucania area of Basilicata in southern Italy and was traditionally made for wedding ceremonies to be eaten with ham, cheese, and preserved vegetables and enjoyed with wine. In local dialect *strazzata* means "to tear with your hands," which is how this pepper-based focaccia was always eaten, and the more pepper it contained the more wine would be consumed at the wedding feast! Locals are very proud of this specialty and even hold annual festivals in its honor.

STRAZZATA LUCANA
Pepper Ring Focaccia

Serves 10–12

½oz/15g fresh yeast (or use approximately
   2¼ tsp/¼oz/7g active-dry yeast, see p.13)
1⅓ cups/320ml lukewarm water
2 cups/9oz/250g white bread flour
1½ cups/9oz/250g durum wheat semolina flour
¼ tsp salt
1 tbsp black pepper

Line a large flat baking tray with parchment paper.

Dissolve the yeast in the lukewarm water.

Mix the flours, salt, and black pepper together. Add the yeast mixture and mix to form a dough. Knead for 10 minutes, cover with plastic wrap, and leave to rest in a warm place for 1 hour, or until doubled in size.

On a lightly floured work surface, roll out the dough into a long sausage shape about 2 feet/63cm in length, flatten lightly with your hands, then form into a ring. You may want to place a small foil-covered bowl in the center so the bread stays in a ring shape. Place on the prepared baking tray, cover with a cloth, and leave to rest in a warm place for 1 hour.

Preheat the oven to 475°F/240°C.

Bake the *strazzata* in the oven for 15 minutes, or until golden brown.

Remove from the oven, leave to cool, then serve.

It's quite common in Italy, especially in rural wine-making areas, to set aside some grapes to make bread or focaccia or buns like these. I remember, at grape harvest time, the baker in our village would make something like this with leftover bread dough. The addition of cinnamon and rosemary really enhance the flavor of the grapes and dough. It's delicious at teatime!

RONDELLE ALL'UVA E ROSMARINO
Grape and Rosemary Buns

Makes 10–12 buns

10½oz/300g grapes, halved
1 tbsp white wine
7 tsp soft light brown sugar
grated zest of ½ lemon
1 tsp ground cinnamon
just under ½oz/12g fresh yeast (or use approximately
    2 heaped tsp/¼oz/6g active-dry yeast, see p.13)
⅔ cup/150ml lukewarm milk
scant 3 cups/12oz/350g white bread flour
needles of 1 rosemary sprig
a little extra virgin olive oil, for brushing

Line a large flat baking tray with parchment paper.

Place the grapes, wine, sugar, lemon zest, and cinnamon in a small bowl and leave to macerate.

Dissolve the yeast in the milk. Place the flour in a large bowl and gradually add the yeast mixture, and mix into a dough. Place the dough on a lightly floured work surface and knead for 10 minutes, then form into a ball, cover with plastic wrap, and leave to rest in a warm place for 15 minutes.

Roll out the dough into a rectangular shape. Scatter the grapes all over, followed by the rosemary needles. Roll the dough lengthways into a long thick sausage and carefully cut into 1in/2.5cm slices. The grapes may escape, but press them back in and form the dough into little basket shapes. Place on the prepared baking tray, brush with a little extra virgin olive oil, cover with a cloth, and leave to rest in a warm place for 30 minutes.

Preheat the oven to 425°F/220°C.

Bake the buns in the oven for 15 minutes until golden brown. Remove from the oven, leave to cool, and enjoy!

I love sun-dried tomatoes but the ones that you buy here are not always the same flavorsome ones I am used to in Italy. So I like to marinate them overnight before eating or using them in my recipes, such as this one, where they top focaccia.

FOCACCIA CON POMODORI SECCHI
Focaccia with Sun-Dried Tomatoes

Serves 6–8

FOR THE DOUGH:
1 quantity of Basic Focaccia
   (see p.56)
semolina or dried
   breadcrumbs, for dusting
FOR THE TOPPING:
1 cup/3½oz/100g
   sun-dried tomatoes
   preserved in oil (with oil
   drained off and reserved)
2 garlic cloves, whole
1 tsp red pepper flakes
1 tsp dried oregano
12 basil leaves
1 tbsp extra virgin olive oil,
   plus extra for drizzling

First prepare the marinated sun-dried tomatoes. Place the drained sun-dried tomatoes in a bowl, reserving the oil. Add the garlic, red pepper flakes, oregano, and basil, then place in an airtight container. Pour in little of the oil from the jar (just enough to cover the tomatoes), cover with a lid, and leave overnight to marinate.

Make the focaccia according to the recipe on p.56.

Preheat the oven to 475°F/240°C. You will need either a rectangular baking pan, about 14¾ x 11in/37.5 x 28cm, or a large round baking pan, about 14½in/37cm in diameter.

On a lightly floured work surface, roll the dough out to roughly the same shape and size as your baking pan.

Warm the baking pan in the oven for about 10 seconds, then remove and sprinkle with some semolina or breadcrumbs. Place the rolled-out dough in the pan and pour the extra virgin olive oil in the middle. Using your fingers, spread the olive oil all over the dough. Leave for 5 minutes, then poke the dough all over with your fingers to make indentations. Top the focaccia with the sun-dried tomato mixture, cover with a cloth, and leave to rest in a warm place for 45 minutes.

Bake the focaccia in the oven for about 20 minutes until evenly golden brown. Check the focaccia occasionally; domestic ovens often color one side more, so turn the pan around accordingly.

Remove from the oven and immediately drizzle a little olive oil all over. Leave to cool, then cut into squares or slices.

This lovely sweet focaccia is ideal at teatime or even for breakfast. I have made it with plums, but you can substitute seasonal fruit like peaches, apricots, apples, pears, or figs. I like to drizzle a little honey over the top and enjoy it with a coffee. The sweetness comes from the fruit and honey, since only a very small amount of sugar is used, so it is a healthy treat. You could enjoy it alongside some soft cheese like creamy Dolcelatte, especially if making with figs.

FOCACCIA DOLCE CON LA FRUTTA
Sweet Focaccia with Fruit

Serves 4–6

⅓oz/10g fresh yeast (or use approximately 1¾ tsp/5g active-dry yeast, see p.13)
generous ¾ cup/200ml lukewarm water
scant 3 cups/12oz/350g white bread flour
½ tsp salt
4 tsp extra virgin olive oil, plus extra for drizzling
1 tbsp runny honey, plus extra for drizzling
3 plums or other fruit
4 tsp Marsala or other sweet wine
extra virgin olive oil, for drizzling
a little granulated sugar, for sprinkling
a little sifted confectioner's sugar, for sprinkling

Lightly grease a shallow rectangular roasting-type pan, about 10½ x 6½in/26 x 17cm, with extra virgin olive oil.

Dissolve the yeast in the lukewarm water.

Mix the flour, salt, olive oil, and honey together. Add the yeast mixture and mix into a dough. Knead for 10 minutes to form a smooth dough. Cover with plastic wrap and leave to rest in a warm place for about 1 hour, or until doubled in size.

Meanwhile, slice the plums or other fruit into segments and place in a bowl with the wine and 1 tablespoon water to macerate.

Place the dough in the prepared pan, drizzle with extra virgin olive oil, and make indentations all over with your fingers. Drain the plums and arrange on top of the dough, then sprinkle with the granulated sugar. Leave to rest in a warm place for 30 minutes, or until doubled in size.

Preheat the oven to 375°F/190°C.

Bake in the oven for about 15 minutes until golden around the edges. Remove, sprinkle with confectioner's sugar, and place under a hot broiler for 2 minutes until caramelized.

Remove from the oven, leave to cool, then slice and serve, drizzled with a little honey, if you like.

PIZZE Pizza

The humble pizza has certainly conquered the world and can be found almost everywhere nowadays, wherever you might be.

This simple dough-based treat, topped with all sorts of delicious ingredients, is loved by all—kids and adults alike—and always a favorite for an informal evening out, children's parties, as street food, or quite simply to enjoy at home.

The origins of pizza are not known for certain, except that it began as street food in Naples. In fact, it probably started as a type of flatbread, which bakers used to test the heat of the oven before baking the daily loaves. To add a little flavor, the bakers would top the flatbreads with some lard, salt, garlic, and herbs. With the introduction of tomatoes in the 1700s, this street food for the poor evolved. It was also a great way for housewives to use up bits of leftovers to top bread dough and make the meal go further.

A century later, a Neapolitan pizza maker created a pizza for Queen Margherita using ingredients of the same colors as the Italian flag for its topping—tomatoes, mozzarella, and basil. The Queen loved it, the combination had been a success, and that is apparently how *Pizza Margherita* came about. Whether this story is true or not, *Pizza Margherita* is still made and loved the world over and its ingredients are used as a basic topping for many other pizzas.

Over the years, pizza has evolved, not only with toppings, but also with shapes like *Calzone* (see p.109), which is basically a folded-over pizza, and *Saltimbocca* (see p.106), whose dough balloons out during baking and is then filled.

Street-food pizza in Italy is commonly sold *al taglio*, by the slice. In pizzerias, it is sometimes served *al metro*, by the meter—long rectangular-shaped pizzas are placed in the middle of the table with different toppings so everyone gets to try a variety—really fun to do when there is a group of you. *Pizzette* or small pizzas (see pp.94–104) are found in bakeries and snack bars and are ideal as food on-the-go.

As with any popular dish, it will inevitably be badly copied. And pizza is no exception; there are so many poorly made versions, whether sold in restaurants, takeout places, or the ready-made store-bought variety. It is amazing how such a simple dish can be made so badly. Of course, there is nothing better than making your own pizza from scratch—it's so simple and economical, it seems crazy not to. Pizza dough can be made in advance and left in the refrigerator, or even frozen, to be used when required. See overleaf for some of my tips for making pizza at home.

TIPS FOR MAKING PIZZA:

• Knead the dough well so it becomes elastic and smooth.

• Make the base as thin as you can.

• Use tomato passata instead of canned tomato sauce since it is ready-sieved.

• Beware of adding too much tomato sauce—this will make the pizza soggy.

• Drizzle a little extra virgin olive oil over the base and topping to help it crisp up.

• Ensure the oven is hot and reaches its temperature before baking the pizza.

BASIC PIZZA DOUGH

Makes 2 round pizzas, about 12½in/32cm in
diameter, or 3 thinner bases, as used for
Pizza Bianca (p.82)

⅓oz/10g fresh yeast (or use approximately
1¾ tsp/5g active-dry yeast, see p.13)
1⅓ cups/320ml lukewarm water
generous 4 cups/1lb 2oz/500g white bread flour
2 tsp salt

Lightly flour a flat baking tray or trays.

Dissolve the yeast in the lukewarm water.

Mix the flour and salt together on a clean work surface, then gradually stir
in the yeast mixture to make a dough. Knead the dough for 10 minutes,
cover with a cloth, and leave to rest for 10 minutes.

Divide the dough into the required number of pieces and knead each
for 2 minutes. Place on the prepared baking tray, cover with a cloth, and
leave to rise in a warm place for 1 hour, or until doubled in size.

Use according to your recipe.

Pizza Bianca is a plain pizza, which I like to top lightly with a little sea salt and some extra virgin olive oil, but if you prefer you can just leave it completely plain or add other flavors (see suggestions below). It is often served instead of bread with antipasto dishes. Make sure you get the pizza dough as thin as you can so it crisps up a bit during baking.

PIZZA BIANCA

Makes 3 round pizzas,
 about 12½in/32cm in diameter

1 quantity of Basic Pizza Dough (see p.80)
coarse sea salt and freshly ground black pepper
extra virgin olive oil
ALTERNATIVE TOPPINGS:
grated Parmesan cheese and sage leaves
olive oil and sliced red chili

Lightly flour 3 large flat baking trays. Prepare the pizza dough according to the recipe on p.80, dividing the dough into 3 equal pieces.

Preheat the oven to 475°F/240°C.

On a lightly floured work surface, roll out each piece of dough as thinly as you can into a circle. Place on the prepared baking trays and sprinkle each pizza base with some salt and pepper and a drizzle of extra virgin olive oil or with one of the alternative toppings.

Bake in the oven for about 10 minutes.

Marinara is a traditional pizza in Naples, topped with tomatoes, garlic, and anchovies, without any cheese. To give this pizza a twist and make it visually appealing, I have used a variety of colored tomatoes readily available in stores and markets these days. It's perfect to make during late summer when local tomato varieties are in abundance.

PIZZA MARINARA
Pizza with Mixed Tomatoes and Anchovies

Makes 2 round pizzas, 12½in/32cm in diameter

1 quantity of Basic Pizza Dough (see p.80)
flour, for rolling
FOR THE TOPPING:
12oz/350g mixed yellow, orange, and red cherry
   tomatoes
2 garlic cloves, finely chopped
¼ cup/60ml extra virgin olive oil, plus extra
   for drizzling
8 anchovy fillets
10 black olives, halved
½ red chili, finely chopped (optional)
pinch of dried oregano
handful of basil leaves

Lightly flour 2 large flat baking trays. Make the pizza dough according to the recipe on p.80, dividing the dough into 2 equal pieces.

Preheat the oven to 475°F/240°C.

Combine all of the topping ingredients together and leave to marinate for about 30 minutes.

On a lightly floured work surface, roll out each piece of dough into a circle about 12½in/32cm in diameter. Place on the prepared baking trays.

Top each pizza base with the tomato mixture and bake in the oven for about 10 minutes. Remove from the oven, drizzle with a little extra virgin olive oil, and serve immediately.

I love this classic pizza with bubbly cheesy deliciousness. You can substitute the cheeses with others if you prefer, such as Dolcelatte, pecorino, or even a hard mozzarella or *ricotta salata*. Go easy on the salt, since some cheeses are quite salty. It's perfect to enjoy with a refreshing glass of beer!

PIZZA AI 4 FORMAGGI
Pizza Topped with 4 Cheeses

Makes 2 round pizzas, about 12½in/32cm in diameter

1 quantity of Basic Pizza Dough (see p.80)
flour, for rolling
FOR THE TOPPING:
extra virgin olive oil, for drizzling
1¾oz/50g Gorgonzola cheese, roughly chopped
1¾oz/50g fontina cheese, roughly chopped
1¾oz/50g provolone (or mature Cheddar) cheese, roughly chopped
½ cup/1¾oz/50g grated Parmesan cheese
salt and freshly ground black pepper

Lightly flour 2 large flat baking trays. Make the pizza dough according to the recipe on p.80, dividing the dough into 2 equal pieces.

Preheat the oven to 475°F/240°C.

On a lightly floured work surface, roll out each piece of dough into a circle about 12½in/32cm in diameter. Place on the prepared baking trays.

Spread a little extra virgin olive oil over each pizza base, top with the cheeses, sprinkle with salt and pepper to taste, and add a little drizzle of olive oil.

Bake in the oven for about 10 minutes until the cheeses melt and bubble.

Although I don't normally cook the tomato before topping a pizza, I make an exception with this particular sauce. I love making it when I have an abundance of tomatoes—so simple—just bake tomatoes in the oven with seasoning and the flavors will infuse beautifully, giving you a rich and flavorsome sauce. I suggest you make lots—any leftover sauce can be used to dress pasta, or it is simply delicious on toast or with some bread.

PIZZA CON SALSA DI POMODORINI AL FORNO
Pizza Topped with Oven-Baked Tomato Sauce

Makes 2 round pizzas, 12½in/32cm in diameter

1 quantity of Basic Pizza Dough (see p.80)
flour, for rolling
FOR THE TOPPING:
1lb 5oz/600g baby plum tomatoes, sliced in half
¼ cup/60ml extra virgin olive oil, plus extra
    for drizzling
3 garlic cloves, squashed
½ red chili, roughly chopped
bunch of basil, roughly torn
sea salt
4½oz/125g fresh mozzarella, roughly chopped
3 tbsp grated Parmesan cheese

Lightly flour 2 large flat baking trays. Make the pizza dough according to the recipe on p.80, dividing the dough into 2 equal pieces.

Preheat the oven to 475°F/240°C.

For the topping, mix together the tomatoes, extra virgin olive oil, garlic, chili, basil, and some salt in a roasting pan and bake in the oven for about 15 minutes, or until the tomatoes have softened.

On a lightly floured work surface, roll out each piece of dough into a circle about 12½in/32cm in diameter. Place on the prepared baking trays.

Top the pizza bases with the tomato sauce, followed by the mozzarella and grated Parmesan. Bake in the oven for about 10 minutes.

Remove from the oven, drizzle with a little extra virgin olive oil, and serve immediately.

Although not entirely gluten-free, this Alpine-inspired pizza uses the healthier alternative flours of spelt and buckwheat to make the base. The simple topping of red onion goes really well with strong, nutty-flavored Gruyère cheese and speck, a smoked salt-cured ham from the northern Alpine regions. Try it for a different pizza.

PIZZA DI GRANO SARACENO
Spelt and Buckwheat Pizza with Speck and Gruyère

Makes 1 round pizza, about 12in/30cm in diameter

FOR THE DOUGH:
¼oz/7g fresh yeast (or use approximately 1¼ tsp/
 ⅛oz/3½g active-dry yeast, see p.13)
¾ cup/180ml lukewarm water
1¾ cups/7oz/200g whole-grain spelt flour
scant ½ cup/1¾oz/50g buckwheat flour
½ tsp salt
FOR THE TOPPING:
2 tbsp extra virgin olive oil, plus extra for greasing
3 thyme sprigs
1 large red onion, sliced
½ cup/2¼oz/60g grated Gruyère cheese
4 slices of speck

Dissolve the yeast in the lukewarm water.

Mix the flours and salt together on a clean work surface. Add the yeast mixture and mix into a dough. Knead the dough for 10 minutes, then form into a ball, wrap in plastic wrap, and leave to rest in a warm place for 1 hour, or until doubled in size.

Preheat the oven to 425°F/220°C. Lightly grease a flat baking tray with a little extra virgin olive oil.

For the topping, heat the extra virgin olive oil in a frying pan over medium heat, add the thyme, and allow to infuse for 1 minute. Add the onion and stir-fry for a minute, then reduce the heat, cover with a lid, and cook until softened. Remove from the heat and set aside.

Roll the dough into a round pizza base about 12in/30cm in diameter and place on the prepared baking tray. Top with the cooked onions and Gruyère, and bake in the oven for 10 minutes. Remove from the oven, arrange slices of speck on top, and serve.

This traditional dish from Abruzzo originated as a poor man's food, using up leftovers to make a nourishing meal. As with most peasant dishes, this is now a recognized local specialty at home and in restaurants and makes a healthy, gluten-free alternative to classic pizza. The base is made with a simple polenta, which is then slow-baked in the oven. The topping is made with local greens—I have opted for broccolini, easily available and tasty. The addition of dried and roasted peppers, available from good delis, adds a lovely, slightly smoky aroma to this delicious rustic dish.

PIZZA E FOJE
Polenta Pizza with Greens

Makes 2 round pizzas, about 8in/20cm in diameter

FOR THE BASE:
extra virgin olive oil, for greasing and drizzling
1 tsp salt
scant 2½ cups/10½oz/300g quick-cook polenta cornmeal
scant ½ cup/1½oz/45g grated Parmesan cheese

FOR THE TOPPING:
14oz/400g broccolini
3 tbsp extra virgin olive oil
2 garlic cloves, whole and crushed
2 dried red peppers, deseeded and roughly chopped in chunks
salt
1 roasted red pepper, drained if preserved in oil, chopped into strips

Preheat the oven to 400°F/200°C. Grease 2 shallow round terracotta dishes or 8in/20cm sandwich cake pans with a little extra virgin olive oil.

Place about about 5 cups/1.2 liters water and the salt in a non-stick saucepan, bring to a boil, then gradually add the polenta, stirring all the time with a spoon or whisk, until well amalgamated. Reduce the heat and, still stirring, cook according to the package instructions. (Quick-cook polenta varieties usually take about 5 minutes.) Remove from the heat and stir in the grated Parmesan. Pour the polenta into the prepared dishes or pans, level out, and drizzle with a little extra virgin olive oil. Bake in the oven for about 50 minutes until slightly golden.

Meanwhile, make the topping. Cook the broccolini in a pan of boiling water for 5 minutes, then drain. Heat the extra virgin olive oil in a frying pan over medium heat, add the garlic and dried peppers, and stir-fry for 2 minutes. Remove the peppers and set aside. Add the broccolini and a little salt to taste and stir-fry for about 5 minutes to allow the flavors to infuse. It's fine if the broccolini is a little overdone. Remove from the heat and discard the garlic.

Top the bases with the broccolini, dried peppers, and roasted red pepper slices. Serve immediately.

Mini *pizzette* are very common in Italian bakeries and takeout places to have as food on the go. This traditional topping of *Pizza Margherita* is always a winner.

PIZZETTE MARGHERITA
Mini Pizzas with Tomato, Mozzarella, and Basil

Makes 5 *pizzette*

½ quantity of Basic Pizza Dough (see p.80)
FOR THE TOPPING:
6 tbsp/90ml tomato passata (or strained tomato
    purée)
extra virgin olive oil, for drizzling
salt
4½oz/125g fresh mozzarella, drained and chopped
a few basil leaves

Lightly flour several large flat baking trays. Make the pizza dough according to the recipe on p.80, dividing the dough into 5 equal pieces, about 3oz/80g each.

Preheat the oven to 475°F/240°C.

Combine the tomato passata or purée with a drizzle of extra virgin olive oil and some salt to taste.

Roll out the balls of dough into small rounds, about 4in/10cm in diameter and place on the prepared baking trays. Spread a little tomato mixture onto each *pizzetta* and top with the mozzarella, a couple of basil leaves, and a drizzle of extra virgin olive oil. Bake in the oven for about 10 minutes.

PIZZETTE DI FUNGHI
Mini Pizzas with Mushrooms

Makes 5 *pizzette*

½ quantity of Basic Pizza Dough (see p.80)
FOR THE TOPPING:
¼ cup/60ml extra virgin olive oil
3oz/80g pancetta, finely sliced
1 garlic clove, finely sliced
½ red chili, finely chopped
needles of 1 rosemary sprig
11oz/320g mushrooms of your choice, finely sliced

Lightly flour several large flat baking trays. Make the pizza dough according to the recipe on p.80, dividing the dough into 5 equal pieces, about 3oz/80g each.

Preheat the oven to 475°F/240°C.

For the topping, heat the extra virgin olive oil in a pan over medium heat, add the pancetta, garlic, chili, and rosemary, and stir-fry for 2 minutes, taking care not to burn the garlic. Add the mushrooms and continue to fry for a further 3 minutes until the mushrooms are cooked. Remove from the heat and set aside.

Roll each ball of dough into small rounds, about 4in/10cm in diameter and place on the prepared baking trays. Top each *pizzetta* with the mushroom mixture and bake in the oven for about 10 minutes.

Prosciutto and arugula go really well together and this is a popular pizza topping. Remember the arugula is put on after the pizza is cooked for a fresh flavor.

PIZZETTE CON PROSCIUTTO E RUCOLA
Mini Pizzas with Prosciutto and Arugula

Makes 5 *pizzette*

½ quantity of Basic Pizza Dough (see p.80)
FOR THE TOPPING:
extra virgin olive oil
5 slices prosciutto
4½oz/125g fresh mozzarella, drained and roughly
    chopped
large handful of arugula

Lightly flour several large flat baking trays. Make the pizza dough according to the recipe on p.80, dividing the dough into 5 equal pieces, about 3oz/80g each.

Preheat the oven to 475°F/240°C.

Roll out the balls of dough into small rounds, about 4in/10cm in diameter and place on the prepared baking trays. Spread a little extra virgin olive oil over each one and top with a slice of prosciutto and some mozzarella. Bake in the oven for about 10 minutes.

Remove from the oven and top with some arugula and a drizzle of extra virgin olive oil.

Scapece is a southern Italian way of cooking zucchini, giving them an extra kick with an infusion of mint and vinegar, then lightly deep-frying before serving them as a salad. It also makes a lovely, different pizza topping.

PIZZETTE ALLA SCAPECE
Mini Pizzas Topped with Zucchini and Mint

Makes 5 *pizzette*

½ quantity of Basic Pizza Dough (see p.80)
FOR THE TOPPING:
vegetable oil, for deep-frying
12oz/350g zucchini (1 large), finely sliced
2 tsp chopped mint leaves
1 garlic clove, finely chopped
1 tbsp white wine vinegar
1 tbsp extra virgin olive oil
salt

Lightly flour several large flat baking trays. Make the pizza dough according to the recipe on p.80, dividing the dough into 5 equal pieces, about 3oz/80g each.

Heat some vegetable oil in a deep pan over a medium-high heat, add the zucchini, and deep-fry until golden brown on both sides. Drain on paper towels. Mix the mint, garlic, vinegar, extra virgin olive oil, and a little salt together, then pour over the zucchini and leave to infuse for 30 minutes.

Preheat the oven to 475°F/240°C.

Roll each piece of dough into small rounds, about 4in/10cm in diameter, place on the prepared baking trays, and top with the zucchini. Bake in the oven for about 10 minutes.

Saltimbocca is another variation in the "pizza family." The dough puffs up in the oven during baking, becoming an oval balloon of hot air! It is then slit and filled, and returned to the oven for a couple of minutes. This typical Neapolitan filling goes really well with this pita-type bread. The secret is to get the dough as thin as you possibly can.

SALTIMBOCCA ALLA SORRENTINA
Saltimbocca with Eggplant

Makes 6

⅓oz/10g fresh yeast (or use approximately
   1¾ tsp/5g active-dry yeast, see p.13)
1⅓ cups/320ml lukewarm water
generous 4 cups/1lb 2oz/500g white bread flour
2 tsp salt
FOR THE FILLING:
3 tbsp extra virgin olive oil
1 whole garlic clove, crushed
1lb 5oz/600g eggplant (1 medium), cut into
   small cubes
10 cherry tomatoes, deseeded and roughly chopped
handful of basil leaves, torn
pinch of salt
4½oz/125g smoked mozzarella, drained and cut into
   small pieces
3 tbsp grated pecorino cheese

Dissolve the yeast in the lukewarm water.

Mix the flour and salt together in a large bowl, add the yeast mixture, and mix into a dough. Knead the dough for about 10 minutes until it is smooth and elastic. Form into a ball, cover with plastic wrap, and leave to rest in a warm place for 1 hour, or until doubled in size.

Meanwhile, make the filling. Heat the extra virgin olive oil in a frying pan over medium heat, add the garlic, and sauté for a minute. Add the eggplant cubes and stir-fry for about 10 minutes until golden and cooked. Stir in the cherry tomatoes and cook for a further 2 minutes. Add the basil leaves and some salt to taste, then remove from the heat, discard the garlic, and set aside.

Preheat the oven to 475°F/240°C and line a flat baking tray with parchment paper.

Divide the dough into 6 equal pieces. Flatten each piece as much as you can by stretching with your hands into a roughly rectangular shape. Place on the prepared tray and bake in the oven for about 10 minutes, or until well risen and golden brown.

Remove from the oven and, using a sharp serrated knife, open the *saltimbocca*. Spread the insides with eggplant filling, mozzarella, grated pecorino, and a drizzle of extra virgin olive oil, then return to the oven for 2 minutes until the mozzarella has melted.

Remove from the oven, close the *saltimbocca*, flatten slightly, and serve.

Calzone, literally translated as "trouser," is basically a pizza that is folded over, and is typical Neapolitan street food. It probably originated for ease of eating while out and about. You can fill it with almost anything you like, rather like pizza toppings. *Calzone* can be made smaller and sometimes known as *panzerotti*, and can be fried instead of baked. In Sicily, *calzone* is known as *cuddurini*.

CALZONE
Basic *Calzone*

Makes 6 *calzone*

⅓oz/10g fresh yeast (or use approximately
   1¾ tsp/5g active-dry yeast, see p.13)
1⅓ cups/320ml lukewarm water
generous 4 cups/1lb 2oz/500g white bread flour
2 tsp salt
extra-virgin olive oil, for brushing
FILLING OPTIONS:
cherry tomatoes, mozzarella, and grated Parmesan
sliced ham and grated Parmesan
ricotta and sliced red onion
tomato, ham, and mozzarella (see p.110)
escarole and pitted black olives (see p.111)

Dissolve the yeast in the lukewarm water.

Mix the flour and salt together on a clean work surface. Add the yeast mixture and mix into a dough. Knead the dough for 10 minutes until smooth and elastic, then form into a ball, cover with plastic wrap, and leave to rest in a warm place for 1 hour, or until doubled in size.

Preheat the oven to 475°F/240°C and line a flat baking tray with parchment paper.

Knock back the dough and divide into 6 equal pieces. Roll each piece into a ball on a lightly floured work surface and flatten and stretch with your hands. With the help of a rolling pin, roll each dough ball out into a circular shape. Place a little of your chosen filling in the middle of each dough circle, keeping a border of 1¼in/3cm all around. Brush the border with water and fold one-half over, pressing down well to make a half-moon shape. Place on the prepared baking tray, brush with a little extra virgin olive oil, and bake in the oven for 12 minutes.

This basic filling for *calzone* is probably the best known and loved, not only in Italy, but all over the world.

CALZONE RIPIENO DI POMODORO, PROSCIUTTO E MOZZARELLA
Calzone Filled with Tomato, Ham, and Mozzarella

Makes 6 *calzone*

⅓oz/10g fresh yeast (or use approximately
   1¾ tsp/5g active-dry yeast, see p.13)
1⅓ cups/320ml lukewarm water
4 cups/1lb 2oz/500g all-purpose flour
2 tsp salt
FOR THE FILLING:
generous ¾ cup/200ml tomato passata
   (or strained tomato purée)
1 tbsp extra virgin olive oil, plus extra for brushing
pinch of salt
6 small slices of cooked ham
4½oz/125g mozzarella, drained, chopped
   into small pieces

Dissolve the yeast in the lukewarm water.

Mix the flour and salt together in a large bowl. Add the yeast mixture and mix into a dough. Knead the dough for 10 minutes until smooth and elastic, then form a ball, cover with plastic wrap, and leave to rest in a warm place for 1 hour, or until doubled in size.

Meanwhile, make the filling. Place the passata or purée in a small bowl and mix with the extra virgin olive oil and salt.

Preheat the oven to 475°F/240°C and line a flat baking tray with parchment paper.

Knock back the dough and divide into 6 equal pieces. Roll each piece into a ball and flatten and stretch with your hands. Using a rolling pin, roll each piece into a circle. Spread a little of the tomato sauce in the middle of each circle, leaving a border of 1¼in/3cm all around. Top with a slice of ham and pieces of mozzarella, brush the border with water, and fold one-half over, pressing down well to make a half-moon shape. Place on the tray, brush with a little olive oil, and bake for about 12 minutes.

This typical southern Italian vegetable is one of my favorites and very popular used to fill *calzone* or even to top pizza in the Neapolitan area. If you can't find escarole then substitute it with green curly endive, which you find in the salad section in stores, or ask your greengrocer.

CALZONE RIPIENO DI SCAROLA
Calzone Filled with Escarole

Makes 6 *calzone*

1 quantity of Basic Calzone dough (see p.109)
FOR THE FILLING:
¼ cup/60ml extra virgin olive oil, plus extra for brushing
2 garlic cloves, whole and squashed
6 anchovy fillets
12 black olives, pitted
3 bunches of escarole, cleaned, leaves separated and roughly chopped
salt and freshly ground black pepper

Make the *calzone* according to the recipe on p.109.

To make the filling, heat the extra virgin olive oil in a pan over medium heat, add the garlic, and sauté for a minute or so until golden. Discard the garlic, add the anchovies and olives, and sauté for another minute until the anchovies dissolve. Stir in the escarole, then cover with a lid and cook over low-medium heat for about 8–10 minutes, until wilted and cooked. Check for seasoning, adding salt and pepper if necessary, then remove from the heat and leave to cool, before using to stuff the *calzone* as per the method on p. 109.

A ricotta filling is very common in *calzone*, especially with red onion. To give it a twist, I have added pieces of salami, which gives a kick to the ricotta.

CALZONE CON RICOTTA E SALAME
Calzone with Ricotta and Salami

Makes 6 *calzone*

1 quantity of Basic Calzone dough (see p.109)
extra virgin olive oil, for drizzling
FOR THE FILLING:
1 cup/9oz/250g ricotta, drained
4½oz/125g mozzarella, drained, roughly chopped
   into small cubes
1¾oz/50g salami, cut into small pieces
¼ cup/1oz/25g grated Parmesan cheese
salt and freshly ground black pepper
2 tsp finely chopped parsley

Make the *calzone* according to the recipe on p.109.

To make the filling, combine all the ingredients together and set aside, before using to stuff the *calzone* as per the method on p. 109.

This is another popular *calzone* filling as well as pizza topping in southern Italy, where the broccoli used is known as *cime di rape*, which in the US are known as broccoli rabe or rapini, and not always easy to find. Broccolini is a good substitute.

CALZONE CON SALSICCIA E BROCCOLI
Calzone with Sausage and Broccoli

Makes 6 *calzone*

1 quantity of Basic Calzone dough (see p.109)
FOR THE FILLING:
1lb 2oz/500g broccoli rabe or broccolini, trimmed
3 tbsp extra virgin olive oil
1 garlic clove, whole and squashed
3 good-quality Italian pork sausages, skin removed,
   crumbled
salt

Make the *calzone* dough according to the recipe on p.109.

To make the filling, blanch the broccoli rabe or broccolini for 2 minutes, then drain and set aside. Heat the extra virgin olive oil in a pan over medium heat, add the garlic, and sweat for 2 minutes, then remove and discard the garlic. Add the crumbled sausage meat, broccoli, and a little salt to the oil and fry over medium heat for 1 minute, stirring. Reduce the heat, cover with a lid, and cook for about 10–15 minutes until the sausage is cooked through and the broccoli is tender but not mushy.

Use to stuff the *calzone* as per the method on p. 109.

TORTE SALATE Savory Pies and Tarts

When thinking of savory pies and tarts, many think of Latin America and its meat pies or France and its quiches. However, Italy has a variety of its own, known as *torte salate*, literally translated as "savory cakes."

Torte salate apparently have age-old roots, dating back to pagan times, when agriculture was an important part of life. To celebrate and give thanks for the first seasonal vegetables, a type of pie would often be made. This was usually around springtime, when all of the lovely fresh greens would come alive in the orchards and gardens, hence classic dishes such as *Torta Pasqualina*, *Erbazzone*, and *Torta Verde* came to being and are still very much part of Italian cooking.

Torte salate was a good way of making bread dough go further, adding fillings of whatever bits of leftovers were available to make a substantial meal for the family. I remember on bread-making day in our house, we would often have a dish like this to enjoy either as part of a meal or to have as a snack. *Torte salate* are common to take on picnics as they contain all the goodness and nourishment you need. They are also popular to serve as an appetizer, with perhaps some other antipasto dishes, usually for special occasions—a large *torta salata* is placed the middle of the table and everyone will have a small slice. These days, I enjoy a slice or two of a *torta salata* for lunch or dinner with a side salad.

Torte salate are also made with pastry; the traditional pastry, sometimes known as *pasta matta*, is a simple mix of flour, salt, extra virgin olive oil, and water, and this is still used today for many tarts like the popular *Erbazzone* (see p.116). It is quick and simple to make, with no need to rest in the refrigerator, and easy to roll out. The lack of butter also makes it a healthier option and its simple flavor makes it perfect to combine with all sorts of savory fillings.

Pastries for savory pies have evolved in Italy and rich shortcrust pastries, known as *pasta frolla*, are also used for tarts and pies.

This savory pie, also known as *scarpazzone*, is a rustic dish from Emilia Romagna. It has humble origins, using up whatever seasonal greens were available, usually from the garden, and perhaps some local cheese to add flavor. It was traditionally cooked in a round copper dish, known in local dialect as *al sol*, in the wood-fired oven where bread was baked. It is still a popular dish in the region and still cooked with local greens. In my version, I have used Swiss chard, including the white stems, which I always leave in dishes to add more flavor. You could substitute spinach. And if you want to make it vegetarian, just omit the prosciutto.

ERBAZZONE
Green Vegetable Pie

Serves 8

FOR THE PASTRY:
scant 3¼ cups/14oz/400g
    all-purpose flour, sifted
1¼ tsp salt
2 tbsp extra virgin olive oil,
    plus extra for greasing
FOR THE FILLING:
3 tbsp extra virgin olive oil,
    plus extra for brushing
2 garlic cloves, finely
    chopped
3½oz/100g prosciutto,
    finely sliced
1¾ cups/5½oz/150g finely
    chopped leeks
2lb 4oz/1kg Swiss chard,
    roughly chopped
salt and freshly ground
    black pepper
1½ cups/5½oz/150g
    grated Parmesan cheese

To make the pastry, combine the flour and salt in a large bowl, add the extra virgin olive oil and a generous ¾ cup/200ml water, and work into a smooth dough. Wrap in plastic wrap and leave to chill while you make the filling.

Heat the olive oil in a large pan over medium heat, add the garlic and prosciutto, and fry, stirring until the prosciutto crisps up. Add the leeks and sweat for 2 minutes. Add the Swiss chard and salt and pepper to taste, and cook over medium-low heat for about 15 minutes, or until tender. Remove from the heat, leave to cool, drain off any excess liquid, and stir in 1 cup/3½oz/100g of the grated Parmesan.

Preheat the oven to 350°F/180°C and lightly grease an 11in/28cm round loose-bottomed tart pan with extra virgin olive oil.

Divide the pastry into two pieces, making one slightly bigger, about 13¼oz/380g. Roll out the bigger piece on a lightly floured work surface and use it to line the prepared pan. Fill the pastry base with the chard filling and sprinkle with the remaining grated Parmesan. Roll out the other piece of pastry, then place over the top and seal the edges. Prick all over with a fork, brush with a little extra virgin olive oil, and bake in the oven for 30–35 minutes until golden. Leave to cool slightly and eat warm.

A delicious rustic savory pie made with bread dough and filled with my favorite southern Italian vegetable. It is delicious enjoyed hot or cold. When I was a young boy, we would take a nutritious pie like this with us on picnics or days out and you didn't really need anything else.

TORTA SALATA CON SCAROLA
Savory Pie with Escarole

Serves 4–6

FOR THE DOUGH:
⅓oz/10g fresh yeast (or use approximately 1¾ tsp/5g active-dry yeast, see p.13)
⅔ cup/150ml lukewarm water
2 cups/9oz/250g white bread flour
pinch of salt
4 tsp olive oil

FOR THE FILLING:
¼ cup/60ml extra virgin olive oil
2 garlic cloves, left whole
4 anchovy fillets
1lb 12oz/800g escarole, sliced into small strips
scant ¼ cup/1oz/25g capers
generous ¼ cup/1¾oz/50g pitted black olives
scant ¼ cup/1oz/25g pine nuts
salt and freshly ground black pepper
2¾oz/75g provolone (or mature cheddar) cheese, cut into small cubes

Dissolve the yeast in the lukewarm water. Combine the flour and salt in a large bowl, add the yeast mixture and olive oil, and mix into a dough. Knead for about 10 minutes until smooth and elastic. Cover with plastic wrap and leave to rest in a warm place for 1 hour, or until doubled in size.

Meanwhile, make the filling. Heat the olive oil in a large frying pan over medium heat, add the garlic and anchovies, and sweat until the anchovies have dissolved and the garlic is golden. Remove and discard the garlic. Add the escarole and fry, stirring for 1 minute. Add the capers, olives, and pine nuts and some salt and pepper to taste and mix well. Reduce the heat to low, cover with a lid, and cook for about 15 minutes until the escarole is tender. Remove from the heat and stir in the cheese.

Meanwhile, preheat the oven to 425°F/220°C and line a 9in/23cm round pie dish with parchment paper.

Divide the dough into two pieces, one a little bigger than the other. Roll out the larger piece on a lightly floured work surface to a roughly round shape and use to line the pie dish. Fill with the escarole mixture. Roll out the remaining dough and place over the top of the filling, pressing down to seal the edges. Prick all over with a fork and bake in the oven for 30–35 minutes until golden all over.

Remove from the oven, rest for 10 minutes, then serve.

Instead of the usual bread dough, I have made a shortcrust pastry for this pie with a little lard, adding richness. If you prefer, you can omit the lard and add extra butter. The *guanciale* (pork cheek) really makes this dish—you could substitute pancetta, but I urge you to get *guanciale*—a good Italian deli will stock it. The pie is simple to make—if you are in a rush, you can buy the pastry ready-made. The excess pastry that lines the pie is folded over and pinched, leaving most of the filling exposed, which looks pretty when served. You can also enjoy this pie cold—in fact, I prefer it the day after when all the flavors have infused nicely. It is quite filling, so I would serve it with perhaps just a side salad. *Illustrated on p.118.*

TORTA SALATA APERTA CON SPINACI, E GUANCIALE E POMODORINI SECCHI

Open Savory Pie with Spinach, *Guanciale*, and Sun-Dried Tomatoes

Serves 4–6

FOR THE PASTRY:
2¾ cups/12oz/350g all-purpose flour
pinch of salt
1 stick/4oz/115g cold unsalted butter, diced
scant ¼ cup/1¾oz/50g cold lard, diced
6 tbsp/90ml ice-cold water

FOR THE FILLING:
1 tbsp extra virgin olive oil
1 small onion, finely diced
7oz/200g *guanciale*, cubed
4 sun-dried tomatoes, roughly chopped
⅓ cup/2¼oz/60g pitted green olives, sliced or left whole, depending on size
1 tbsp tomato paste mixed with a splash of white wine
freshly ground black pepper
1lb 2oz/500g spinach
2 eggs, beaten
3 tbsp grated Parmesan cheese
2 cherry tomatoes, halved
1 egg yolk, beaten

For the pastry, combine the flour and salt in a large bowl. Add the butter and lard and rub them into the flour until it resembles breadcrumbs. Add enough of the ice-cold water to make a smooth dough, wrap in plastic, and leave to chill for at least 30 minutes.

Preheat the oven to 400°F/200°C and line a 9½in/24cm round ceramic or terracotta flan dish with parchment paper.

Heat the oil in a large pan over medium heat, add the onion and *guanciale*, and sweat until the onion has softened. Stir in the sun-dried tomatoes, olives, and tomato paste and season with a little black pepper. Add the spinach and cook for a minute or so until the spinach has wilted. Remove from the heat and leave to cool. Remove excess oil, if necessary. Stir in the beaten eggs and Parmesan and set aside.

On a lightly floured work surface, roll out the pastry to a circular shape about ½in/1cm thick and use to line the flan dish. Make sure you have excess pastry all around the edges. Pour the filling inside the pastry base and fold over the excess pastry, pinching at regular intervals. Most of the filling will be visible. Arrange the sliced tomatoes on top and bake in the oven for 50 minutes. About halfway through the cooking time, brush the pastry with egg yolk and continue to bake until cooked and golden.

Remove from the oven, leave to rest for 5 minutes, then slice and serve. This can also be eaten cold.

This delicious pie is made with a pastry known as *pasta matta*, which translates as "crazy pastry!" I don't know why it has this bizarre name, but it is a pastry often made in Italy for both sweet and savory delicacies. Quick and simple to make, it is easy to roll out, since it doesn't tend to crack, and is much lighter due to the low fat content. The filling of ricotta and zucchini combines really well and the addition of grilled zucchini in a lattice pattern makes this a very pretty pie indeed, as well as being delicious to eat! Perfect served with a mixed salad for a light lunch or it can be enjoyed cold on a picnic. *Illustrated on p.119.*

TORTA RUSTICA CON ZUCCHINE E RICOTTA
Zucchini and Ricotta Pie

Serves 6

FOR THE PASTRY:
scant 3¼ cups/14oz/400g
    all-purpose flour, sifted
pinch of salt
6 tbsp/90ml extra virgin
    olive oil
⅔ cup/150ml sparkling
    water
FOR THE FILLING:
3 large zucchini
1 tbsp extra virgin olive oil
1½oz/40g pancetta, cut
    into small cubes
1 small onion,
    finely chopped
1 cup/9oz/250g ricotta
1 egg
handful of basil leaves,
    roughly torn
scant ½ cup/1½oz/45g
    grated Parmesan cheese
salt and freshly ground
    black pepper
egg wash (see p.13)

To make the pastry, combine the flour and salt in a large bowl or work surface, make a well in the center, add the extra virgin olive oil, and gradually add the sparkling water, mixing to form a soft dough. Form into a ball, wrap in plastic, and leave to rest at room temperature for about 20 minutes.

Cut 2 of the zucchini lengthways into ¼in/5mm thick slices. Heat a grill pan over high heat and grill the zucchini on each side until they soften, then remove and set aside.

Preheat the oven to 375°F/190°C. Line a 9½in/24cm round pie dish with parchment paper.

Finely slice the remaining zucchini. Heat the extra virgin olive oil in a pan, add the pancetta and onion, and fry over medium heat, stirring until the pancetta is nearly crispy and the onion has softened. Add the sliced zucchini, reduce the heat to low, cover with a lid, and cook for about 5 minutes until the zucchini has softened. Remove from the heat, drain any liquid, and leave to cool.

Combine the ricotta, egg, basil, Parmesan, and pancetta mixture in a bowl. Season with salt and black pepper to taste.

On a lightly floured work surface, roll out the pastry to about ⅟₁₆in/2mm thick and use to line the pie dish, making sure you have some excess pastry around the edges. Fill with the filling mixture. Place the zucchini strips in a lattice pattern over the filling, then fold over the excess pastry, pinching it at regular intervals. Brush the pastry and zucchini with egg wash and bake for about 25 minutes until golden.

Remove from the oven, rest for 5 minutes, slice, and serve.

Savory pies like this one were often made when I was a child in Italy, especially on bread-making days when we had leftover dough; whatever produce was around would be used as a filling. This pie is ideal to make during spring when fresh fava beans are available, however, it is just as good with frozen ones. If you are using fresh, remember to remove the skin after shelling. The addition of preserved artichokes really gives a kick to this dish, and with the added potatoes, this is a substantial meal in itself.

TORTA SALATA CON FAVE E CARCIOFI
Savory Pie with Fava Beans and Artichokes

Serves 4–6

FOR THE DOUGH:
⅓oz/10g fresh yeast (or use
    approximately 1¾ tsp/5g
    active-dry yeast, see p.13)
⅔ cup/150ml lukewarm
    water
2 cups/9oz/250g white
    bread flour
pinch of salt
2 tbsp/1oz/25g unsalted
    butter, room temperature,
    cut into pieces
FOR THE FILLING:
10½oz/300g potatoes,
    peeled and sliced into
    ½in/1cm rounds
salt and black pepper
2 tbsp extra virgin olive oil,
    plus extra for drizzling
1 banana shallot,
    finely chopped
5½oz/150g fava beans,
    shelled and peeled
1 x 10oz/285g jar of
    preserved artichokes
    (discard the oil)
2½oz/70g prosciutto,
    chopped
3 egg yolks, beaten
3 tbsp milk
scant ½ cup/1½oz/45g
    grated Parmesan cheese
1 egg yolk, beaten

Dissolve the yeast in the lukewarm water. Combine the flour, salt, and butter in a large bowl. Make a well in the center, gradually pour in the yeast mixture, and mix well to form a soft dough. Knead on your work surface for 10 minutes, then form into a ball, cover with a cloth, and leave to rise in a warm place for 1 hour, or until doubled in size.

Preheat the oven to 425°F/220°C and line a 9in/23cm round pie dish with parchment paper. Lightly grease a baking tray.

Place the potato rounds on the prepared baking tray, sprinkle with some salt and pepper, and drizzle with some extra virgin olive oil. Roast in the oven for about 10 minutes until golden and cooked through. Remove from the oven and set aside.

Heat the oil in a frying pan over medium heat, add the shallots and fava beans, and sauté until the fava beans are soft. Remove from the heat and leave to cool. Once cool, combine with the artichokes, proscuitto, egg yolks, milk, Parmesan, and some salt and pepper to taste. Set aside.

Divide the dough in half. Roll out one piece on a lightly floured work surface and use to line the pie dish, making sure there is some overlapping the sides. Fill the pie with the vegetable filling, then roll out the other piece of dough and use to cover the pie, folding the overlap over the top and sealing well so that the filling does not escape. Prick all over with a fork and bake in the oven for about 35 minutes until golden. About halfway through the cooking time, brush the top of the pie with some beaten egg yolk.

Remove from the oven, leave to rest for 5 minutes, and serve. This is delicious served hot or cold.

This tasty, rustic mushroom pie is made with a variety of flours, making the dough light and full of flavor. The filling is simply made with cultivated white mushrooms, but you could substitute the wild varieties in season if you prefer. It is tied like a *fagotto* or a knapsack, which makes it look really pretty when presented at the table. It is delicious eaten hot or cold with a salad.

FAGOTTO DI FUNGHI CON FARINE MISTE
Mixed Grains Mushroom Pie

Serves 4–6

FOR THE BREAD DOUGH:
just under ½oz/12g
    fresh yeast (or use
    approximately 2 heaped
    tsp/¼oz/6g active-dry
    yeast, see p.13)
⅔ cup/150ml lukewarm
    water
2 cups/9oz/250g all-
    purpose flour
scant ¼ cup/1oz/25g
    buckwheat flour
scant ¼ cup/1oz/25g
    polenta cornmeal
5 tbsp/1oz/25g Italian
    chickpea flour
1 tsp salt
1 egg
FOR THE FILLING:
3 tbsp extra virgin olive oil
2¼oz/60g pancetta, diced
1 leek, finely sliced
3 thyme sprigs, leaves only
1lb 5oz/600g mushrooms
    of your choice, sliced
salt and freshly ground
    black pepper
splash of white wine
egg wash (see p.13)

Dissolve the yeast in the lukewarm water. Combine the flours and salt in a large bowl, add the yeast mixture and egg, and mix well into a dough. Knead for 10 minutes, cover with plastic wrap, and leave to rest in a warm place for about 1 hour, or until doubled in size.

To make the filling, heat the extra virgin olive oil in a pan over high heat, add the pancetta, leek, and thyme, and fry for 3–4 minutes, stirring. Stir in the mushrooms, then add some salt and pepper. Add the wine and allow it to evaporate, about 1 minute. Reduce the heat to medium, cover with a lid, and cook for 5 minutes.

Preheat the oven to 350°F/180°C. Line a pie dish or a flat baking tray with parchment paper.

Roll out the dough into a thin square sheet big enough to line the pie dish or baking tray and place in the prepared dish or tray. Prick the dough all over with a fork. Place the mushroom filling in the center, then take the 4 corners of the dough and make into a parcel (see photo). Tie with kitchen twine and brush all over with egg wash. Bake in the oven for 45 minutes.

Remove from the oven, leave to rest for 5 minutes, then slice and serve.

This lovely tart is the savory counterpart of the sweet version so loved in Naples at Easter time (see p.175). If you looked at it not knowing it was savory, you could easily mistake it for the classic sweet one. Deliciously tasty and rich, it is made with a variety of cheeses and cured meats—a great way to use up leftovers! Use whatever you have—you don't have to use the same as in this recipe. Although it is delicious hot, it is best sliced and served when left to rest for a while.

PASTIERA SALATA
Savory Neapolitan Wheat Tart

Serves 8

FOR THE PASTRY:
scant 3⅔ cups/15oz/450g all-purpose flour, sifted
pinch of salt
scant ½ cup/1½oz/45g grated Parmesan cheese
½ cup/120ml olive oil, plus extra for greasing
3 egg yolks
about ¼ cup/60ml cold water
FOR THE FILLING:
10½oz/300g jar or can of *grana cotta*, pre-cooked
    wheat (sold in Italian delis or online)
generous ¾ cup/200ml milk
3 tbsp/1½oz/40g unsalted butter
1¼ cups/10½oz/300g ricotta
4 egg yolks
3oz/80g provolone (or mature Cheddar) cheese, cut
    into small cubes
3oz/80g fontina cheese, cut into small cubes
¾ cup/3oz/80g grated Parmesan cheese
¼ cup/¾oz/20g grated pecorino cheese
3½oz/100g Neapolitan salami, cut into small cubes
2¼oz/60g mortadella, roughly chopped

To make the pastry, combine the flour, salt, and Parmesan in a large bowl. Mix in the olive oil and egg yolks and gradually add enough cold water to form a smooth dough. Wrap in plastic and leave to rest at room temperature while you make the filling.

Place the wheat, milk, and butter in a saucepan and cook over medium heat, stirring with a wooden spoon until the milk is absorbed and it is a

creamy consistency. Remove from the heat and allow to cool.

Preheat the oven to 350°F/180°C. Grease an 11in/28cm loose-bottomed tart pan with olive oil and dust with flour.

Mash the ricotta with a fork, mix it with the cooled wheat mixture, and stir in the egg yolks, cheeses, cured meats, and some salt and pepper. Go easy with the salt; the cheeses and meats are quite salty already.

On a lightly floured work surface, roll out the pastry to a thickness of ¼in/5mm and use to line the prepared tart pan. Fill with the mixture. Reroll the remaining pieces of pastry and cut into thin strips, then place them in a criss-cross pattern over the filling.

Bake in the oven for 40–45 minutes until the cheeses have melted and the filling has puffed up nicely and is golden brown all over.

Remove from the oven and rest for at least 20 minutes before serving.

I don't normally encourage people to buy pastry, but puff pastry is quite a tricky one to master and get right. So for this recipe I allow myself to cheat and use store-bought all-butter puff pastry, which is widely available and actually very good. In Italy, it is common to fill a *torta salata* or *rotolo* with mixed bitter greens known as *erbette*, which I have never been able to find elsewhere. So I have opted for rainbow chard, which is a variety of brightly colored Swiss chard. It is beautiful to look at, tastes delicious, and works well with puff pastry. The potatoes not only add a little bulk but combine well with the chard, together with delicious provolone cheese. If you can't find provolone, substitute a good-quality mature Cheddar. Serve the *rotolo* with a tomato salad for a light meal, or it can be eaten cold as a snack or for a picnic.

ROTOLO CON BIETOLE
Rainbow Chard Puff Pastry Roll

Serves 4–6

4 tbsp/2oz/60g unsalted butter
1 small onion, finely chopped
1lb 5oz/600g rainbow chard, finely sliced (including stalks)
salt and freshly ground black pepper
1 large potato, peeled and thinly sliced with a mandolin or cheese grater
2 tbsp grated Parmesan cheese
1lb 2oz/500g all-butter puff pastry
1¾oz/50g provolone cheese, shaved or grated
egg wash (see p.13)

Melt the butter in a large pan, add the onion, and sauté over medium heat until softened. Stir in the chard and season with salt and pepper. Cover with a lid, reduce the heat, and cook for about 10 minutes, until the chard is tender but not mushy (the stalks should be "al dente"). Stir in the potatoes and cook for a further 2 minutes. Remove from the heat and leave to cool, then stir in the Parmesan.

Preheat the oven to 375°F/190°C and line a large flat baking tray with parchment paper.

Roll out the pastry on a lightly floured work surface into a rectangular shape about ⅟₁₆–⅛in/2–3mm thick. Place the filling about one-quarter of the way in from one of the longer sides of the pastry sheet, then arrange the provolone on top, and carefully fold over the pastry to make a roll, sealing the ends and bringing them together to form a ring. If necessary, brush some egg wash to seal. Place on the prepared baking tray.

Using a small sharp knife, make incisions at about 1½–2in/4–5cm intervals and brush with egg wash. Bake in the oven for about 40 minutes until golden.

Remove from the oven, leave for 3–4 minutes, then slice along the incisions and serve. This can also be eaten cold.

This is a lovely combination of an American pot pie with a classic Italian chicken filling. The title *alla Cacciatora*, translated as "in the style of the hunter," suggests it was probably first made with game birds or rabbit. As with many Italian dishes, it also has roots in *cucina povera* (poor-man's food), where people used whatever they had on hand; in this case poultry, enriched with whatever vegetables and herbs were available to make it go further. Chicken *Cacciatora* is made all over Italy in different ways and usually eaten with bread. It makes a wonderful pie filling. The pastry is a basic shortcrust, but if you prefer, you can use a sheet of store-bought puff pastry for the lid.

TORTA SALATA CON POLLO ALLA CACCIATORA
Chicken *Cacciatora* Pie

Serves 4

FOR THE PASTRY:
2 cups/9oz/250g all-purpose flour, sifted
9 tbsp/4½ oz/125g cold unsalted butter, cubed
¼ cup/60ml cold water
FOR THE FILLING:
¼ cup/60ml extra virgin olive oil
1 small onion, finely chopped
½ red chili, finely chopped
1 celery stalk, finely chopped
1 carrot, finely chopped
1 red bell pepper, finely chopped
salt and black pepper
15oz/450g skinless chicken breast, cut into chunks
2 thyme sprigs
scant ½ cup/100ml white wine
1 tbsp tomato paste mixed with 2 tbsp warm water
6oz/170g cherry tomatoes, halved
9oz/250g button mushrooms, sliced
scant ½ cup/100ml chicken stock
1 small egg, beaten

To make the pastry, place the flour into a large bowl, add the butter, and rub it in until it resembles breadcrumbs. Gradually add enough of the cold water to make a smooth dough. Wrap in plastic wrap and leave to chill for at least 30 minutes.

To make the filling, heat the extra virgin olive oil in a large deep pan over medium heat, add the onion, chili, celery, carrot, and pepper, and sauté for 5 minutes. Rub salt and pepper all over the chicken pieces, add them to the pan, and fry until sealed all over. Add the thyme, increase the heat, pour in the wine, and allow to evaporate, about 3–4 minutes. Reduce the heat to low, stir in the tomato paste mixture, cherry tomatoes, mushrooms, and stock, then cover with a lid and gently cook for 25 minutes. Remove from the heat and leave to cool slightly.

Meanwhile, preheat the oven to 400°F/200°C.

When the chicken is ready, pour into a 9½in/24cm round pie dish. On a lightly floured work surface, roll out the pastry to a thickness of about ⅛in/3mm and place on top of the filling, pinching the edges over the sides of the pan to seal. Brush all over with egg wash, then make an incision on the top and bake in the oven for about 30–35 minutes, until golden and heated through. Serve.

These Umbrian flatbreads take their name from the stone they were traditionally cooked on known as *testo*—a flat tile that was placed on the fire to heat up and enable the circles of dough to be cooked. Quick and cheap, rural families made these flatbreads instead of heartier breads and often in large quantities, which were stored in a special container placed by the fireplace to be kept warm and ready for when the family returned home. Nowadays the flatbreads are sliced open and filled with local cured meats and cheese. They are so popular in Umbria, particularly around Perugia, that annual *sagre* (food festivals) are held in their honor. I like to make them with oozing fontina cheese and ham and serve them as Italian grilled cheese sandwiches to my girls. They are equally delicious with pesto and Parmesan or other fillings such as sausage, vegetables, greens, or whatever else you prefer.

TORTA AL TESTO
Umbrian Flatbreads

Makes 8

just under ½oz/12g
    fresh yeast (or use
    approximately 2 heaped
    tsp/¼oz/6g active-dry
    yeast, see p.13)
1⅓ cups/320ml lukewarm
    water
generous 4 cups/1lb 2oz/
    500g white bread flour,
    sifted
pinch of salt
1 tbsp extra virgin olive oil
FILLING OPTIONS:
cooked ham
fontina cheese, roughly
    sliced
basil pesto
grated Parmesan cheese

Line a large flat baking tray with parchment paper.

Dissolve the yeast in the lukewarm water.

Combine the flour and salt in a large bowl. Add the extra virgin olive oil and yeast mixture and mix into a dough. Knead for 10 minutes, cover with plastic wrap, and leave to rest in a warm place for about 2 hours, or until doubled in size.

Divide the dough into 8 pieces, about 3½oz/100g each. On a lightly floured work surface, roll out each piece of dough into an 8in/20cm round. Prick all over with a fork.

Heat a griddle or non-stick frying pan until very hot. Place a dough round in the pan and cook on both sides until golden brown. Repeat with the remaining dough rounds.

Preheat the oven to 400°F/200°C.

When the flatbreads are cool enough to handle, slit them open along one side and fill them with ham and cheese or pesto and Parmesan, or whatever combination you prefer. Close them and place on the prepared baking tray. Bake in the oven for a few minutes until the cheese has melted and the flatbreads have warmed through. Serve immediately.

These simple, lovely polenta-floured parcels make a delicious lunch served with a salad or as a snack at any time. They are perfect for lunchboxes or as food on the go.

FAGOTTINI CON POMODORINI SECCHI E OLIVE
Sun-Dried Tomato and Olive Parcels

Makes 6

¼oz/7g fresh yeast (or use approximately 1¼ tsp/
    ⅛oz/3½g active-dry yeast, see p.13)
⅔ cup/150ml lukewarm water
scant 1¼ cups/5½oz/150g white bread flour
1 cup/4½oz/125g polenta cornmeal
1 tsp salt
¾ cup/3oz/80g sun-dried tomatoes, chopped
6 pitted green olives, roughly chopped
a little extra virgin olive oil, for brushing

Line a flat baking tray with parchment paper.

Dissolve the yeast in the lukewarm water. Combine the flours and salt in a large bowl, add the yeast mixture, and mix into a dough. Knead for 10 minutes, form into a ball, cover with plastic wrap, and leave to rest in a warm place for 2 hours, or until doubled in size.

Divide the dough into 6 equal pieces, about 3oz/80g each. On a lightly floured work surface, roll out each piece into a roughly oval shape, place the tomatoes and olives in the center of each, and roll up along the short side. Place the rolls seam-side down on the prepared baking tray, cover with a cloth, and leave to rest in a warm place for 1 hour.

Preheat the oven to 400°F/200°C.

Bake in the oven for 20 minutes, brush with a little extra virgin olive oil, and continue to bake for a further 10 minutes until lightly golden. Leave to cool slightly and serve warm. They are also good cold.

PAN DOLCI Sweet Breads

When I think of *pan dolci*, my taste buds immediately go into action and my mouth waters. I love the aroma, texture, and flavor of delicate sweet leavened breads like brioche, *panettone*, and *danubio*—not too sweet or sickly rich, they are perfect to enjoy for breakfast, tea, or after meals.

Pan dolci are sweet leavened breads that have been enriched with eggs, butter, and perhaps other ingredients. The dough has a softer, finer texture than bread because the fat weakens the gluten in the flour. For this reason, enriched doughs require a longer kneading and rising time. Because sugar is often added to *pan dolci* and this inhibits yeast growth, these breads are usually made with a much larger quantity of yeast. Most *pan dolci* take a long time to make, but they really are worth the effort and wait. There is nothing nicer than taking a freshly baked batch of brioche out of the oven—the smell, appearance, and taste are definitely worth the time spent. To save on labor, I recommend using a stand mixer when making *pan dolci*.

Pan dolci are popular all over Italy and many regional varieties exist. Many are seasonal, like the popular *panettone* and *pandoro* at Christmas and *colomba* at Easter. These seasonal treats are all industrially made now and available not only in Italy but in stores all over the world. In bakeries and cake shops in Italy, artisanally made *pan dolci* are found, and these tend to be of a much higher quality than the mass-produced variety. As with bread, *pan dolci* are part of tradition and culture, and most came about as *cucina povera* (poor man's food), where leftover bread dough was enriched with a little sugar or honey. Apparently this is how *panettone* came about at Christmastime, when poorer families added a little dried fruit to bread dough as a special sweet treat for this important feast.

This simple, light sweet bread can be eaten at any time. It is delicious toasted and served with jam for breakfast or teatime. It was traditionally made with lard, but to make it lighter, I have used butter. In Tuscany, slices are often dipped into Vin Santo or coffee.

PAN DOLCE TOSCANO
Tuscan Sweet Bread

Serves 6–8

FOR THE DOUGH:
just under ½oz/12g fresh yeast (or use approximately
    2 heaped tsp/¼oz/6g active-dry yeast, see p.13)
⅔ cup/150ml lukewarm water
2 cups/9oz/250g all-purpose flour, plus
    generous ¾ cup/3½oz/100g more for kneading
2 egg yolks
6 tbsp/2¾oz/75g superfine sugar
3½ tbsp/1¾oz/50g unsalted butter, softened
grated zest of 1 orange
grated zest of 1 lemon
pinch of ground cinnamon
pinch of salt
confectioner's sugar, for dusting

Grease an 8in/20cm round cake pan and line with parchment paper.

Dissolve the yeast in the lukewarm water. Place 2 cups/9oz/250g flour on your work surface, add the yeast mixture, and mix into a dough. Knead for 10 minutes, form into a ball, wrap in plastic, and leave to rest in a warm place for 1 hour, or until doubled in size.

Meanwhile, whisk the egg yolks, sugar, and butter together in a bowl until light and creamy. Add the zests, cinnamon, and salt.

Place the risen dough on the work surface, flatten with your hands, and gradually work the egg mixture into the dough, gradually adding the extra flour until a soft dough has formed. Place the dough into the prepared pan, cover with a cloth, and rest in a warm place for a further 1 hour.

Preheat the oven to 375°F/190°C.

Bake in the oven for 30 minutes until golden. Remove from the oven, leave to cool, then tip out of the pan and dust with confectioner's sugar.

Multi-colored and multi-flavored, this beautiful brioche bread will surely impress any table at teatime.

TRECCIA COLORATA
Braided Sweet Bread

Serves 12–15

1oz/25g fresh yeast (or use approximately
    4½ tsp/½oz/15g active-dry yeast, see p.13)
scant ½ cup/100ml lukewarm water
generous 4 cups/1lb 2oz/500g white bread flour
1½ tsp salt
2 tbsp sugar
3 eggs, beaten
5 tbsp/2½oz/70g unsalted butter, melted and cooled
⅓ cup/1oz/25g unsweetened cocoa powder
2½ tbsp dark chocolate chips
grated zest of 1 orange
2 tbsp orange liqueur
⅓ cup/1½oz/40g chopped walnuts
2 pinches of saffron powder, diluted in
    2 tsp milk
3 tbsp golden raisins, soaked in rum to cover
confectioner's sugar, for sifting (optional)

Line a large baking tray with parchment paper. Dissolve the yeast in the lukewarm water.

Mix the flour, salt, and sugar together in a large bowl. Make a well in the center and pour in the yeast mixture, eggs, and melted butter, and mix well to form a dough. Knead for 5 minutes, then cover with plastic wrap and leave to rest in a warm place for 1 hour, or until doubled in size.

Divide the dough into 3 equal pieces, about 9¾oz/275g each. Take one piece and mix in the cocoa powder, chocolate chips, orange zest, and suit yourself with the orange liqueur. You may find you need more or less, so add this gradually. Knead until everything is well incorporated, then roll out into a long sausage about 1½ feet/45cm in length and set aside.

Take another piece of dough, add the walnuts and saffron mixture, and proceed as above.

Take the third piece of dough and add the raisins. You may find you do not need all of the rum, so add this gradually.

Form the 3 sausage shapes into a braid, place on the prepared baking tray, and rest in a warm place for a further 1 hour, or until doubled in size.

Preheat the oven to 400°F/200°C.

Bake the braid in the oven for 25 minutes. Remove from the oven, leave to cool, then sprinkle with confectioner's sugar, if desired, and serve.

This *pan dolce* (sweet bread) is a typical delicacy of the Tuscan town of Lucca. Its name is taken from the Latin *buccellatum*, meaning mouthful. It was eaten by the ancient Romans. Over time, it has evolved to include currants and aniseed. It is usually made into a ring or sausage shape and is especially popular during the Lucca festivals in September. I was very pleasantly surprised when I first made this cake; not too sweet, a slight aroma of aniseed, and packed full of currants, which I love. It's ideal for breakfast or at any time with a coffee.

BUCCELLATO DI LUCCA
Aniseed and Currant Ring Cake

Serves 8

1 cup/5½oz/150g zante currants
4 tsp aniseed liqueur (like Sambuca)
1oz/25g fresh yeast (or use approximately
    4½ tsp/½oz/15g active-dry yeast, see p.13)
1 tsp honey
⅔ cup/150ml lukewarm water
4 cups/1lb/480g white bread flour, sifted
¾ cup/5½oz/150g sugar
2½ tbsp aniseeds
1 egg
2 tbsp/1oz/25g unsalted butter, melted and cooled
egg wash (see p.13)

Grease a 9½in/24cm ring pan and line with parchment paper. Soak the currants in the aniseed liqueur, adding enough lukewarm water to cover. Set aside.

Dissolve the yeast and honey in the lukewarm water. Mix the flour, sugar, and aniseeds together in a large bowl. Add the egg, butter, drained currants, and yeast mixture, and mix until well incorporated and a dough is formed. Knead for 2 minutes, form into a ball, cover with plastic wrap, and leave to rest in a warm place for 2 hours, or until doubled in size.

On a lightly floured work surface, roll out the dough with your hands and form into a long sausage shape to fit into the pan. Cover with plastic wrap and leave to rest in a warm place for 1½ hours, or until doubled in size.

Preheat the oven to 350°F/180°C.

Brush the cake with egg wash and bake in the oven for 50 minutes until the top is golden brown. Remove from the oven, leave to cool, then tip out of the pan, slice, and serve.

I love *Pandoro* and so does my family, so I had to include this alternative Italian Christmas cake in this book. Unlike *Panettone* (see p.145), it does not contain any dried fruit and often it is preferred for this reason—my daughter Chloe would eat *Pandoro* every day if she could! Making *Pandoro* at home does take time, so begin the day before; it needs to rest in the refrigerator overnight as well as rise before and after. The result is certainly worth the effort, ending with a less sweet cake than the industrially produced store-bought variety. It does dry out quicker than the store-bought ones, so it's best eaten within a couple of days, however, I don't think that will be a problem—well, not in my house anyway!

PANDORO

Serves 10

¾oz/20g fresh yeast (or use approximately
   3½ tsp/⅓oz/10g active-dry yeast, see p.13)
¼ cup/60ml lukewarm milk, plus 3 tbsp extra
⅔ cup/4½oz/130g sugar
1 egg yolk
generous 3¾ cups/1lb/480g all-purpose flour, sifted
3 eggs
1½ sticks/6oz/170g unsalted butter, cut into small
   cubes and softened at room temperature
seeds of 1 vanilla bean
1 tsp salt
1½ tbsp/¾oz/20g melted unsalted butter, plus
   extra for greasing
confectioner's sugar, for dusting

Dissolve ½oz/15g of the fresh yeast (or 2⅔ teaspoons/¼oz/7g of the active-dry yeast) in ¼ cup/60ml of the lukewarm milk. Stir in 2½ tablespoons of the sugar and 1 egg yolk. Add a scant ½ cup/1¾oz/50g of the flour and stir until it is well incorporated. Cover with plastic wrap and leave to rest for about 1 hour, or until it is doubled in volume.

Dissolve the remaining ⅛oz/5g fresh yeast (or 1 teaspoon/3g active-dry yeast) in the 3 tablespoons lukewarm milk. Add this to the above mixture. Stir in the remaining ½ cup/3½oz/100g sugar and 1 egg. Stir in about 1⅔ cups/7oz/200g of the flour and 2 tablespoons/1oz/25g of the softened butter until it is well incorporated. Cover with plastic wrap and leave to rest for 1 hour, or until it has doubled in volume.

Add the remaining flour (a generous 1¾ cups/8oz/230g), 2 eggs, and the vanilla and salt to the mixture, and mix until everything is well incorporated. Lightly grease a large bowl and place the sticky dough inside it. Cover with plastic wrap and leave to rest in a warm place for 1 hour, or until doubled in size, then leave to chill overnight (12–15 hours).

Place the dough on a floured work surface and, using a rolling pin, roll out into a square. Place the remaining butter cubes (10 tbsp/5oz/140g) into the center of the dough square and fold in the 4 corners, sealing well over the butter so it does not escape. Press down with your hands and roll into a rectangular shape. Fold over 3 times, then place on a plate or board, cover with plastic wrap, and leave to chill for 20 minutes.

Fold the dough over again 3 times, then gently press down and leave to chill for 15 minutes. Repeat the process and leave to chill for a further 15 minutes.

On a lightly floured work surface, roll out the dough into a square. Fold in the 4 corners and form into a ball. Spread a little of the melted butter all over the ball of dough. With the remaining melted butter, grease a large 8-point star-shaped 8½x4x6in/750g *pandoro* pan (available online), place the dough inside, cover with plastic wrap, and leave to rest in a warm place for about 4 hours, or until the dough has risen to the top of the pan.

Preheat the oven to 325°F/160°C.

Bake the *pandoro* on the bottom shelf of the oven at this temperature for 15 minutes. Reduce the oven temperature to 300°F/150°C, cover the top of the *pandoro* with foil, and continue to cook for 40 minutes until cooked through. Check by inserting a wooden skewer; if it comes out clean, the cake is done, if it is still moist, cook for a little longer.

Remove from the oven, leave to cool, then turn out onto a flat plate. When completely cool, dust with confectioner's sugar and serve.

The traditional Italian Christmas cake, *Panettone*, though delicious, is quite a lengthy process to make at home. I have therefore come up with this quick method to make the mini version so often found in coffee shops these days and not always good. Made with instant yeast and only left to rise once, they are quick and simple to make at any time. They are not too sweet either, so they are perfect to enjoy with a cappuccino for breakfast.

PANETTONCINI VELOCI
Quick Mini *Panettone*

Makes 10 mini *panettone*

generous 4 cups/1lb 2oz/500g white bread flour
pinch of salt
2 x ¼oz/7g envelopes instant yeast
seeds of 1 vanilla bean
½ cup/3½oz/100g superfine sugar
3 eggs, beaten
⅔ cup/150ml milk
1 stick/4oz/115g unsalted butter,
    melted and cooled
scant ½ cup/3½oz/100g ricotta, drained
about ½ cup/2½oz/70g mixed dried fruit,
    chopped if large
½ cup/2½oz/70g pine nuts
grated zest of 1 orange
grated zest of 1 lemon

Grease and line a 10-hole mini *panettone* pan with parchment paper (or you can use 3in/7cm terracotta pots lined with parchment paper).

Mix the flour, salt, yeast, vanilla, and sugar together in a large bowl. Make a well in the center and stir in the eggs and milk, then add the butter. In a separate bowl, combine the ricotta, dried fruit, pine nuts, and citrus zests. Add this to the rest of the ingredients and combine well, mixing with your hands. The dough will be sticky but don't worry. Cover with a cloth and leave to rest in a warm place for about 1½ hours, or until doubled in size.

Preheat the oven to 400°F/200°C.

Place dollops of the mixture into the prepared pan and bake in the oven for about 25 minutes until golden brown.

Remove from the oven, leave to cool, then turn out of the pan and enjoy.

There are many varieties of *pan dolce* that contain dried fruit in every region of Italy and this is my version. It may take a little time to make but it is worth the effort. The addition of mixed tropical fruit cuts through the richness and gives the cake a very pleasant flavor. I shape it into a coil to give it variety from the classic ring shape into which a lot of *pan dolci* are made. The smell during cooking is irresistible, but do wait for the cake to cool before serving.

PAN DOLCE ALLA FRUTTA SECCA ESOTICA MISTA
Mixed Tropical Fruit Bread

Serves 10

¾oz/20g fresh yeast (or use approximately
   3½ tsp/⅓oz/10g active-dry yeast, see p.13)
scant ½ cup/100ml lukewarm milk
5 cups/1lb 5oz/600g white bread flour,
   plus extra for flouring
9oz/250g mixed tropical dried fruit, chopped (about
   1½–1¾ cups, depending on the variety)
scant ½ cup/100ml Vin Santo (or other sweet wine)
1½ tsp salt
⅔ cup/4½oz/130g superfine sugar
grated zest of 1 lemon
3 eggs
7 tbsp/3½oz/100g unsalted butter, melted and
   slightly cooled

Line a 9½in/24cm round cake pan with parchment paper.

Dissolve the yeast in 5 tablepoons/70ml of the milk. Place a scant 1 cup 3½oz/100g of the flour in a large bowl, add the yeast liquid, and mix into a dough. Form into a ball, cover with plastic wrap, and leave to rest in a warm place for 1½ hours, or until it has doubled in size.

Place the dried fruit in a bowl, pour in the Vin Santo, and leave to soak.

Place the risen dough, remaining flour, salt, sugar, zest, eggs, melted butter, and remaining 2 tablespoons of milk in a large bowl and work into a dough. It will be sticky to start with, but continue mixing and kneading. You will find it easier to knead on a lightly floured work surface. Return the dough to the bowl, cover with a cloth, and leave to rise in a warm place for 2 hours, or until doubled in size.

On a lightly floured work surface, roll out the dough into a roughly rectangular shape about ¼in/5mm thick. Scatter the drained dried fruit all over, then roll the dough lengthways into a sausage shape, securing well by pressing the dough with your fingers to ensure the filling does not escape. Wrap the large sausage around into a coil shape and carefully place in the lined cake pan. Cover with a cloth and leave in a warm place for a further 1 hour.

Preheat the oven to 400°F/200°C.

Bake the fruit bread in the oven for 1 hour. If you find that it browns quite quickly, place foil over the top for the duration of baking.

Remove from the oven, leave to cool, then turn out of the pan, slice, and enjoy!

The addition of yogurt and olive oil gives this brioche loaf a lovely light texture. It is perfect for breakfast, either plain or toasted, and especially delicious spread with Nutella. The lack of butter and only a little sugar makes this a very healthy option, and it is so much nicer than the store-bought variety, which I find very sweet. The dough can be made by hand but it will be a little sticky to handle—don't worry, this is perfectly normal. If you prefer, you can make it in a stand mixer, which will do all the sticky work for you in no time.

PAN BRIOCHE
Brioche Loaf

Serves 4–6

¾oz/22g fresh yeast (or use approximately a scant
    4 tsp/just under ½oz/11g active-dry yeast, see p.13)
scant ½ cup/100ml lukewarm milk, plus extra for
    brushing
3¾ cups/15oz/450g white bread flour
pinch of salt
3 tbsp sugar
½ cup/120ml organic plain yogurt
¼ cup/60ml olive oil
2 eggs
1 tsp honey
1 tsp vanilla extract
sanding sugar, for topping

I use a silicone 9½ x 5in/24 x 13cm loaf pan so I don't have to grease it, but for other types, lightly grease with some oil.

Dissolve the yeast in the lukewarm milk.

Mix the flour, salt, and sugar together in a large bowl. Add the yogurt, olive oil, eggs, honey, vanilla, and yeast mixture, and mix well to form a dough. Cover with plastic wrap and leave to rest in a warm place for 4 hours.

Place the dough on a lightly floured work surface and place in the prepared loaf pan. Leave to rest in a warm place for a further 1 hour, or until doubled in size.

Preheat the oven to 375°F/190°C.

Brush the top of the brioche with a little milk and sprinkle with sanding sugar. Bake in the oven for 30 minutes until well risen and golden. Remove from the oven, leave to cool, then tip out of the pan and slice.

This soft, light, sweet brioche is popular in Naples. It originates from Austria and was first made in a Neapolitan pastry shop in the 1920s, after the owner married a woman from the Saltzburg region. Authentically known as *buchteln* and filled with apricot jam, the Italians renamed it *danubio*. This recipe is filled with a delicious homemade custard cream, but it can also be filled with any jam or pieces of chocolate. It's probably worth making double the quantity—once you start to eat you can't stop! There is a savory version on p.50.

DANUBIO DOLCE CON CREMA PASTICCIERA
Sweet Brioche Filled with Custard Cream

Serves 4–6

FOR THE DOUGH:
just under ¼oz/6g fresh
  yeast (or approximately
  1 tsp/3g active-dry yeast,
  see p.13)
½ cup/120ml lukewarm
  milk
scant 2½ cups/10½oz/
  300g white bread flour
1 tsp salt
1 tbsp sugar
seeds of ½ vanilla bean
  (reserve the bean)
grated zest of 1 lemon
1 egg, beaten
2 tbsp/1oz/25g melted
  unsalted butter, cooled
egg wash (see p.13)
FOR THE CUSTARD CREAM:
scant ½ cup/100ml milk
2 tbsp heavy cream
piece of lemon rind
½ vanilla bean (use the
  bean from above)
2 egg yolks
5 tsp sugar
1½ tbsp cornstarch

Lightly grease an 8in/20cm round sandwich cake pan and line with parchment paper.

Dissolve the yeast in the lukewarm milk. Mix the flour, salt, sugar, vanilla seeds, and zest together in a large bowl. Add the yeast mixture and mix until it is well amalgamated. Add the egg and butter and work into a soft dough. Knead the dough on a lightly floured work surface for about 10 minutes until smooth. Cover with plastic wrap and leave to rest in a warm place for 2 hours, or until doubled in size.

Meanwhile, make the custard. Combine the milk, cream, lemon rind, and vanilla bean in a small pan and infuse over gentle heat for about 5 minutes, stirring occasionally.

Beat the egg yolks and sugar together in a bowl until light and fluffy, then beat in the cornstarch. Remove the pan from the heat and whisk in the egg mixture. Return the pan to low heat and whisk continuously until you obtain a thick, creamy consistency. Pour into a bowl or plate, cover with plastic wrap, and leave to cool.

Divide the dough into 15 pieces, each weighing about 1oz/25g. Shape each into a ball, then flatten into small circles with a rolling pin. Place 1 teaspoon of the custard cream into the center of each, sealing the edges around it and rolling to form small balls. Arrange the balls next to each other in the prepared pan, cover with plastic wrap, and rest in a warm place for 1 hour, or until doubled in size.

Preheat the oven to 350°F/180°C.

Brush egg wash all over the top of the brioche and bake in the oven for 20 minutes until golden brown. Remove from the oven, leave to cool slightly, then tear and share.

Col tuppo in Sicilian dialect means "putting hair in a bun" and the shape of these brioche rolls is reminiscent of this traditional hairstyle. These rolls are served all over Sicily in cafés and pastry shops, filled with classic almond granita or ice cream for a delicious summer breakfast. They are wonderful on their own, too, with a coffee, and are best eaten on the day they are made. Otherwise, wrap them in plastic or foil to keep them fresh for a few more days. The rising times are quite long (best to start the day before you want to serve), but it's worth the wait! If you have a stand mixer, I suggest you use it for this recipe—it will be much easier to incorporate the butter.

BRIOCHE COL TUPPO
Sicilian Brioche

Makes 6

¼oz/7g fresh yeast (or approximately 1¼ tsp/ ⅛oz/3½g active-dry yeast
2 tbsp lukewarm milk
2 cups/9oz/250g white bread flour, sifted
3 tbsp sugar
1 tsp salt
3 eggs
1½ sticks/6oz/170g unsalted butter, diced and softened
egg wash (see p.13)
good-quality ice cream, to serve (optional)

Line a large flat baking tray with parchment paper and dissolve the yeast in the lukewarm milk.

Mix the flour, sugar, and salt together in a large bowl or stand mixer. Mix in the yeast mixture and the eggs, one at a time, then very gradually mix in the butter, combining well between each addition, otherwise you will get lumps of butter in the mixture. This will take quite a long time, especially if you are beating by hand.

If the mixture has been in the mixer, transfer it to a large bowl, cover with plastic wrap, and leave to rest in a warm place for 4 hours. After this time, the mixture will have tripled in size. Chill for about 12 hours, but no longer than 18 hours. Overnight is best for this.

Place the dough on a lightly floured work surface and, using your hands, roll into a large sausage shape, then divide into 6 equal portions. Remove a small piece from each portion and roll both pieces into balls. Flatten the larger piece and make an indentation, then place the smaller ball into the indentation. Arrange the dough onto the prepared baking tray, brush all over with egg wash, and leave to rest in a warm place for a further 2 hours.

Preheat the oven to 350°F/180°C.

Bake for 25 minutes. Remove from the oven and place on a wire rack. If desired, gently tear off the top, fill with ice cream, and enjoy!

Dove-shaped breads can be traced back to the ancient Greeks and Egyptians, and biblically the dove has always been a symbol of peace. There are many legends about the origins of this sweet bread, but *Colomba* was first produced industrially in the 1930s by the Milanese company, Motta, makers of the famous *Panettone* (see p.145). Wanting to create a similar cake for Easter, this dove-shaped version with candied fruits and almonds was born, and has since become a must-have on the Italian Easter table. This wonderful, delicate sweet bread can of course be enjoyed at any time of the year and the silicone dove-shaped mold can be purchased online. Since it is not too sweet, it is delicious for breakfast. It is best eaten freshly made—wrap leftovers in foil and store in an airtight container. The store-bought ones do last longer, but are not as delicious. You will need to start this recipe the day before.

COLOMBA
Dove-Shaped Easter Cake

Serves 12

FOR THE STARTER DOUGH:
⅓oz/10g fresh yeast (or use approximately 1¾ tsp/5g active-dry yeast, see p.13)
½ cup/120ml milk, lukewarm
¾ cup/3⅓oz/95g all-purpose flour, sifted

FOR THE CAKE:
½oz/13g fresh yeast (or use approximately 1½ tsp/5g instant yeast, see p.13)
⅓ cup/2½oz/70g sugar, plus 1 tsp
2 eggs
1 egg yolk
1 tsp vanilla extract
1 stick/4oz/115g unsalted butter, softened, plus extra for greasing
2 cups/9oz/250g all-purpose flour, sifted, plus extra for flouring
½ tsp salt
grated zest of 1 lemon
grated zest of 1 orange
4½oz/130g good-quality candied citrus peel, diced

FOR THE TOPPING:
⅓ cup/1oz/25g ground almonds

First, make the starter dough. Dissolve the yeast in the lukewarm milk. Place the flour in a large bowl, add the yeast mixture, and stir with a wooden spoon until it is well incorporated. Cover with plastic wrap and leave at room temperature for 12 hours, or overnight.

The next day, mix the yeast and 1 teaspoon sugar together in a small bowl. Whisk the eggs, yolk, and remaining sugar together in a large bowl until light and creamy. Add the yeast mixture and vanilla extract, then add the starter dough and butter, and beat gently with a wooden spoon or spatula until everything is well incorporated. Fold in the flour and salt. Turn out onto a lightly floured work surface and knead by hand for 10 minutes. Incorporate the zests and candied peel, and knead for 1 minute until well amalgamated. Place the dough in a lightly buttered bowl, cover with plastic wrap, and rest in a warm place for 2 hours, or until doubled in size.

Carefully place the dough in an 11in/2lb 4oz/1kg silicone dove-shaped baking mold (or a 5½ cup/1.3 liter capacity cake pan), cover with plastic wrap, and leave to rest in a warm place for 1 hour.

Meanwhile, make the topping. Whisk all the ingredients together in a large bowl to form a smooth paste. Set aside.

Preheat the oven to 400°F/200°C.

Spread the paste all over the top of the dove, scatter with the whole almonds, and sprinkle with a little sifted

¼ cup/1¾oz/50g sugar
1 egg white
½ tbsp cornstarch

TO DECORATE:
scant ¼ cup/1oz/25g whole
　　almonds
confectioner's sugar

confectioner's sugar. Place the mold on a flat baking tray and bake in the oven for 15 minutes. Reduce the oven temperature to 350°F/180°C, cover the top with foil, and continue to bake for a further 15 minutes.

Remove from the oven, leave to cool, then carefully take the dove out of the mold and place it on a plate or board.

This almond tea bread was meant to be made into a ring shape, but during the testing of the recipe, we found we didn't have quite enough dough, so we changed it into a horseshoe, which actually looks really nice and different. The ricotta filling adds moisture and the cocoa powder gives it a good color when cut into slices. It's lovely to enjoy at teatime.

PAN DOLCE MANDORLATO A FORMA DI ZOCCOLO DI CAVALLO

Almond Horseshoe

Serves 6–8

FOR THE DOUGH:
just under ½oz/12g fresh yeast (or approximately 2 heaped tsp/¼oz/6g active-dry yeast
½ cup/120ml lukewarm milk
3⅓ cups/14oz/400g white bread flour, plus extra for flouring
1 tsp salt
⅓ cup/2½oz/70g sugar
1 tsp vanilla extract
grated zest of 1 large orange
1 egg
1 egg yolk
3½ tbsp/1¾oz/50g unsalted butter, melted

FOR THE FILLING:
scant ½ cup/3½oz/100g ricotta
3 tbsp sugar
generous ½ cup/1¾oz/50g unsweetened cocoa powder
3½oz/100g amaretti cookies, crushed
1 cup/3½oz/100g slivered almonds, chopped, plus extra for sprinkling
1 egg
1 tbsp Marsala or sweet wine
egg wash (see p.13)

Line a large flat baking tray with parchment paper. Dissolve the yeast in the lukewarm milk.

Mix the flour, salt, and sugar together in a large bowl. Add the remaining ingredients, including the yeast mixture, and mix into a smooth dough. Knead for 5 minutes, then form into a ball, wrap in plastic, and leave to rest in a warm place for 1 hour, or until doubled in size.

Meanwhile, make the filling. Mix the ricotta and sugar together in a bowl until creamy. Stir in the cocoa powder until it is well incorporated, then stir in th the cookies, almonds, egg, and Marsala. Cover with plastic wrap and leave to chill for about 30 minutes, or until required.

On a lightly floured work surface, roll out the dough into a roughly rectangular shape of about 1½ x 1 ft/45 x 30cm or as thin as you can get it. Spread the filling all over, leaving a small border of about 1½in/4cm. Carefully roll from the long side, sealing the edges well with the help of a little water. Form into a horseshoe shape and make small incisions with a sharp knife around the sides. Carefully place on the prepared baking tray and leave to rest in a warm place for a further 30 minutes.

Preheat the oven to 400°F/200°C.

Brush with egg wash, scatter with slivered almonds, and bake in the oven for about 30 minutes until golden all over. If it starts to brown before the end of cooking time, cover with foil. Leave to cool before eating.

Buondi means "good day"—what a fabulous name for the Italian equivalent of croissants! These remind me of my youth when every café in Italy would sell them for breakfast. Nowadays you can buy industrially produced Buondi in shops in Italy, but the flavor and smell of baking them at home is beyond comparison! They are not difficult to make, but their resting time is long, so begin the day before, and if you want them freshly made for a breakfast treat, it will be an early morning start!

BUONDÌ
Italian Croissants

Makes 20

FOR THE STARTER:
⅓oz/10g fresh yeast (or use approximately
   1¾ tsp/5g active-dry yeast, see p.13)
scant ¼ cup/50ml lukewarm water
generous ¾ cup/3½oz/100g white bread flour
FOR THE MIXTURE:
½ cup/3½oz/100g superfine sugar
2 tsp honey
⅓ cup/80ml milk
8 egg yolks
3⅓ cups/14oz/400g white bread flour
14 tbsp/7oz/200g unsalted butter, softened
grated zest of 1 lemon
grated zest of 1 orange
2 drops of orange extract
seeds of 1 vanilla bean
1½ tsp salt
FOR THE SYRUP:
¾ cup/5½oz/150g sugar
sprinkles or pearl sugar, for topping

First, make the starter dough. Dissolve the yeast in lukewarm water. Put the flour in a large bowl, add the yeast mixture, and mix to a smooth dough. Form the dough into a ball, cover with plastic wrap, and leave to rest in a warm place for 1 hour.

Mix the sugar, honey, and milk together in a large bowl. In a separate bowl, whisk the egg yolks until creamy, then gradually add them to the sugar mixture, alternating with flour until everything is well incorporated. Add the butter (if necessary give the butter a quick whisk so it is soft

and gooey), citrus zests, orange extract, vanilla, salt, and starter dough, and mix well by hand for about 10 minutes until everything is well incorporated. Cover with plastic wrap and leave to rest in a warm place for 2 hours. After this time, leave the dough to chill for 12 hours.

The next day, divide the dough into 20 pieces, each weighing roughly 1¾oz/50g. Shape into small fat sausages about 2¾in/7cm long and 1¾in/4.5cm wide, and place in individual mini loaf pans lined with parchment paper. Leave to rest in a warm place for 4 hours.

Preheat the oven to 350°F/180°C.

Bake the *buondi* in the oven for about 15 minutes until golden brown, then remove from the oven and leave to cool.

Meanwhile, make the syrup. In a small saucepan, bring a scant ½ cup/100ml water to a boil with the sugar. Boil for about 1 minute until the sugar has dissolved. Remove from the heat and leave to cool slightly.

Remove the *buondi* from the pans and place on a wire rack. Brush with the cooled syrup and top with sprinkles or pearl sugar.

CROSTATE Sweet Pies and Tarts

Crostate are sweet tarts, which to many Italians, including myself, evoke happy childhood memories. Traditionally home-baked by mamma or nonna, filled with homemade jam, and topped with criss-crossed strips of pastry, they were always a welcome teatime treat.

Pasta frolla (shortcrust pastry) is generally used as a basis for most sweet tarts. Basic ingredients of flour, butter, sugar, and egg yolks are used to make this popular rich and sweet pastry. Over the years, Italians have evolved their approach to pastry, and puff pastry as well as filo are popular choices for many desserts. I normally like to make my own pastry; however, I do make an exception when it comes to puff pastry or filo, since they are quite labor intensive. As with bread, Italians are now experimenting with different grains, and pastries made from buckwheat or spelt or rice flour are not uncommon.

Pasta frolla is really simple to make and if you make it in a stand mixer, it is even quicker. As soon as the dough is ready, make sure you wrap it tightly in plastic wrap and leave it to rest and cool down in the refrigerator for at least 30 minutes. When I make pastry, I like to make a large quantity so I can freeze what I don't need and use it to make another *crostata* at another time.

Fillings vary, too, including the classic *Crostata di Marmellata* (Jam Tart, see p.169) and the *Crostata di Ricotta e Nutella* (Ricotta and Nutella Tart, see p.161). Ricotta is used a lot in Italian desserts and *crostate* are no exception. It provides an excellent filling, combining well with other ingredients, and is also less fatty than cream. *Crema pasticciera* (custard cream) is another favorite filling; it is homemade and often flavored with lemon or chocolate, depending on your *crostata*. Italians love fruit, so seasonal fruit-topped *crostate* are a popular choice.

TIPS FOR MAKING PASTRY:

• Work in a cool, dry kitchen.

• Use good-quality butter or other fat, since the flavor of the fat will affect the flavor of the pastry.

• Work quickly and lightly; overworked pastry can be tough.

• When rolling out the dough, use only a little flour to dust your work surface; any additional flour can make the dough dry.

• Always leave your dough to rest in the refrigerator.

• **BLIND BAKING** (or baking blind) means to cook the pastry before adding any filling. When you have lined the tart pan with the dough, place a circle of parchment paper a little larger than the diameter of the pastry base and place over the dough. Top with a layer of ceramic pie weights (or you can use dried beans) and bake in a preheated oven for about 15 minutes, then carefully remove the weights and parchment paper and continue to bake for a further 5 minutes or so until the pastry becomes golden.

There is nothing better than the taste of homemade custard. It is so much more nutritious and less sweet than the store-bought varieties and is also simple to make. *Crema pasticciera* is widely used in Italy for a lot of desserts and cakes in preference to cream. This is my sister Adriana's recipe, which forms the basis of custard fillings for the tarts in this chapter.

CREMA PASTICCIERA FATTA IN CASA
Thick Homemade Custard

Makes enough to fill the pastry bases in this book

2 cups/500ml whole milk
seeds of 1 vanilla bean
6 egg yolks
½ cup/3½oz/100g sugar
½ cup/2¼oz/60g all-purpose flour, sifted

Place the milk and vanilla seeds in a small saucepan over medium heat until the milk is hot but not boiling.

Meanwhile, whisk the egg yolks and sugar together in a bowl until light and fluffy. Gradually add the flour and continue to whisk until it is incorporated. Pour in the hot milk and continue to whisk for a few seconds, making sure there are no lumps—if there are, continue to whisk until they have disappeared.

Return the mixture to the pan over medium heat and cook, stirring constantly with a wooden spoon, until the custard begins to thicken. At this point, increase the heat and stir quickly, but do not allow it to boil or burn. If it begins to bubble, immediately remove the pan from the heat.

To cool the custard quicker, pour it into a heatproof bowl or container, cover with a lid or plastic wrap, and set aside until cool.

Ricotta is a very popular filling in Italy for both sweet and savory pies and tarts. Lighter than a lot of other creamy cheeses, it is ideal in desserts. I find ricotta especially delicious combined with chocolate, hence the idea of adding a thin layer of Nutella—the ricotta cuts through the sweetness and makes for a really yummy tart. It is lovely to serve as a dessert or simply at teatime.

CROSTATA DI RICOTTA E NUTELLA
Ricotta and Nutella Tart

Serves 6

FOR THE PASTRY:
2 cups/9oz/250g all-purpose flour, sifted
pinch of salt
1 stick/4oz/115g cold unsalted butter, cut into small pieces, plus extra for greasing
½ cup/3½oz/100g superfine sugar
2 egg yolks
FOR THE FILLING:
1⅔ cups/14oz/400g ricotta
1 tbsp sugar
1 tbsp Marsala or other sweet wine
1¾oz/50g milk chocolate, roughly chopped (optional)
½ small jar (about 3½oz/100g) of Nutella

To make the pastry, combine the flour and salt in a large bowl. Add the butter and rub it in until it resembles breadcrumbs. Add the sugar, then add the egg yolks and mix well to form a smooth dough. Wrap in plastic wrap and leave to chill for at least 30 minutes.

Meanwhile, preheat the oven to 350°F/180°C. Grease a 9½in/24cm round tart pan with a little melted butter, then dust with flour.

For the filling, mix the ricotta, sugar, Marsala, and chocolate pieces, if using, together in a bowl. Cover with plastic wrap and leave to chill until required.

On a lightly floured work surface, roll out the dough to a thickness of ¼in/5mm and use to line the prepared tart pan. Trim off the excess pastry and set aside. Spread a thin layer of Nutella over the bottom of the pastry, followed by the ricotta mixture. Reroll the remaining pastry and cut it into strips. Place over the top of the tart, making a lattice pattern.

Bake in the oven for 40 minutes until golden. Eat warm or leave to cool.

This is a lovely rustic tart made with dried apricots, which are cooked to make a jam. It reminds me of the homemade *crostata* made by family and friends when I was growing up in Italy. An extra layer of unsweetened pastry is added in the middle to cut through the sweetness of the apricot filling. You can substitute the apricots with prunes and use walnuts or slivered almonds instead of pine nuts, if you prefer.

CROSTATA DI ALBICOCCHE SECCHE
Dried Apricot Tart

Serves 6

FOR THE PASTRY:
1 egg
2 egg yolks
2¾ cups/12oz/350g all-purpose flour, sifted
pinch of salt
10 tbsp/5oz/140g cold unsalted butter,
   cut into small pieces
FOR THE FILLING:
scant 2 cups/9oz/250g dried apricots
scant 1 cup/6¼oz/180g superfine sugar
juice of ½ lemon
grated zest of 1 lemon
⅓ cup/1½oz/45g pine nuts
egg wash (see p.13)
confectioner's sugar, for sprinkling (optional)

Soak the dried apricots for the filling in enough lukewarm water to cover.

To make the pastry, beat the egg and yolks together and set aside. Mix the flour and salt in a large bowl, add the butter, and rub it in until it resembles breadcrumbs. Add the eggs and mix well to form a smooth pastry. Form into a ball, wrap in plastic, and leave to chill until required.

Meanwhile, make the filling. Drain the apricots and place the water in a saucepan, together with the sugar, and stir over low heat until the sugar has dissolved. Add the apricots, increase the heat, bring to a boil, and cook over medium-high heat for about 25 minutes, or until it is a jam-like consistency. Remove from the heat and stir in the lemon juice and zest.

Preheat the oven to 350°F/180°C. Line an 8in/20cm pie dish with parchment paper.

Divide the pastry into 3 pieces, making one slightly larger. On a lightly floured work surface, roll out the larger piece and use it to line the prepared pie dish. Fill with half of the apricot filling and sprinkle with half of the pine nuts. Roll out another piece of dough the same size as the base of the pie dish and place this pastry round over the apricots. Fill with the remaining apricot mixture and sprinkle with the remaining pine nuts. Roll out the remaining pastry, cut out strips with a pastry cutter, and form a lattice shape over the top. Carefully fold over any excess pastry that is hanging over the edge. Brush the pastry all over with egg wash and bake in the oven for about 45 minutes, or until golden.

Remove from the oven and leave to cool. Sprinkle with confectioner's sugar, if desired, and serve.

I love semolina pudding, which forms the filling of this sophisticated peach tart. You can use other fruit, such as strawberries, or a selection of fruit, like berries, kiwi, pineapple, plums, or whatever you prefer. This tart makes a lovely dinner party dessert. *Illustrated overleaf.*

CROSTATA DI CREMA DI SEMOLINA E PESCHE
Tart with Semolina Cream and Peaches

Serves 6–8

FOR THE PASTRY:
generous ¾ cup/3½oz/
    100g all-purpose flour
⅔ cup/3½oz/100g rice
    flour
7 tbsp/3½oz/100g cold
    unsalted butter, cut into
    small pieces
3 tbsp sugar
1 egg

FOR THE FILLING:
¾oz/20g gelatin leaves or
    2 envelopes/½oz/14g
    unflavored gelatin
    powder
4 cups/1 liter milk
1 vanilla bean, split in half
    lengthways
⅔ cup/3½oz/100g durum
    wheat semolina flour
½ cup/3½oz/100g sugar
generous ¾ cup/200ml
    heavy whipping cream
about 5–6 ripe peaches,
    finely sliced
sifted confectioner's sugar,
    for sprinkling

First, make the pastry. Sift the flours into a large bowl, add the butter, and rub it in until it resembles breadcrumbs. Stir in the sugar, then add the egg, and mix well to form a smooth dough. Form into a bowl, wrap in plastic, and leave to chill for at least 30 minutes.

Preheat the oven to 350°F/180°C.

On a lightly floured work surface, roll out the dough to a thickness of about ⅛in/3mm and use to line an 8½in/22cm loose-bottomed tart pan. Blind bake (see p.159) for about 20 minutes. Remove from the oven, leave to cool, then carefully remove from the pan and place on a flat plate.

Meanwhile, make the filling. Soften the gelatin leaves or dissolve the powder in enough warm water to just cover. Place the milk and vanilla bean into a saucepan and bring to a boil. Stir in the semolina, reduce the heat, and cook for 10 minutes, stirring constantly. Add the sugar and stir until dissolved. Strain the gelatin leaves, if using, and add them (or the powdered gelatin mixture) to the pan. Leave to cool, then remove the vanilla bean. Whip the cream until stiff, and fold it into the semolina mixture.

Pour the mixture into the pastry, arrange the sliced peaches on top, and sift with confectioner's sugar. Serve.

This lovely strawberry tart looks very pretty and the combination of lemon and strawberries is delicious. It is perfect to make in late spring/early summer when local strawberries are in abundance and at their best. *Illustrated overleaf.*

CROSTATA DI FRAGOLE E LIMONE
Strawberry and Lemon Tart

Serves 8

FOR THE PASTRY:
2 cups/9oz/250g all-purpose flour, sifted,
    plus extra for flouring
pinch of salt
9 tbsp/4½oz/125g cold unsalted butter,
    plus extra for greasing
¾ cup/2¾oz/75g sifted confectioner's sugar,
    plus extra for sprinkling
grated zest of 1 lemon
2 egg yolks, slightly beaten
FOR THE FILLING:
1 quantity of Thick Homemade Custard (see p.160)
grated zest of 1 lemon, plus extra for sprinkling
generous 4 cups/1lb 5oz/600g strawberries, sliced
    or left whole, depending on size

First, make the pastry. Mix the flour and salt together in a large bowl, add the butter, and rub it in until it resembles breadcrumbs. Stir in the confectioner's sugar and lemon zest, then add the egg yolks and mix well to form a smooth pastry. Form into a ball, wrap in plastic wrap, and leave to chill for at least 30 minutes.

Preheat the oven to 350°F/180°C. Lightly grease an 8½in/22cm loose-bottomed tart pan with butter and dust with flour.

Make the filling. Make the custard according to the recipe on p.160, and add the lemon zest.

Roll out the pastry on a lightly floured work surface and use to line the prepared pan. Blind bake (see p.159) for about 25 minutes. Remove from the oven and leave to cool, then carefully transfer to a flat plate.

Fill the cooked pastry with the cooled custard and decorate with strawberries and a sprinkling of lemon zest and confectioner's sugar.

These pretty tarts are fun to make and you can use your imagination when it comes to decorating them—in fact, get the kids involved, they will love it! I like to use a selection of jam—apricot, raspberry, plum, peach—or whatever I have in the pantry. Homemade jam is best, otherwise go for a good-quality brand that does not contain too much sugar.

CROSTATINE DI MARMELLATA
Jam Tarts

Makes 6

FOR THE PASTRY:
2 cups/9oz/250g all-purpose flour
9 tbsp/4½oz/125g cold unsalted butter,
    cut into small pieces, plus extra for greasing
¾ cup/2¾oz/75g sifted confectioner's sugar
seeds of ½ vanilla bean
2 egg yolks
jam of your choice or a selection (a 14oz/400g
    jar will be plenty)
egg wash (see p.13)

Sift the flour into a large bowl, add the butter, and rub it in until it resembles breadcrumbs. Stir in the confectioner's sugar and vanilla, then add the egg yolks and mix to a smooth dough, working quickly to avoid the dough getting warm. Form the dough into a ball, wrap in plastic wrap, and leave to chill for at least 30 minutes, or until required.

Preheat the oven to 350°F/180°C. Lightly grease 6 round 4½in/12cm loose-bottomed tartlet pans with butter, then dust with flour.

On a lightly floured work surface, roll out the dough to a thickness of ¼in/5mm and use to line the prepared tartlet pans. Lightly prick the bottoms with a fork and fill each with jam. Gather up the remaining bits of pastry, roll out, and cut out strips or shapes to place over the top. Brush the pastry with a little egg wash.

Place the pans on a flat baking tray and bake in the oven for 20–25 minutes until golden.

Remove from the oven, leave to cool, and carefully remove from the pans.

Like puff pastry, filo is a type of pastry that I don't normally make at home. It takes time and I find good-quality store-bought ones absolutely fine to use. This extremely simple but delicious dessert will surely impress your guests. The thick homemade custard goes really well with the berries. Use whatever is in season and what you prefer.

CROSTATA AI FRUTTI DI BOSCO E CREMA PASTICCIERA

Filo Pastry Tart with Custard and Mixed Berries

Serves 4–6

1 quantity of Thick Homemade Custard (see p.160)
6 square sheets ready-made filo pastry
3 tbsp/1½oz/40g unsalted butter, melted
scant 1 cup/3½oz/100g mixed berries (such as raspberries, blueberries, and blackberries)

Make the custard according to the recipe on p.160 and leave to cool.

Preheat the oven to 375°F/190°C. Grease an 8in/20cm sandwich cake pan with some of the melted butter.

Trim the filo pastry into squares of about 9½in/24cm, if necessary. Line the prepared cake pan with a sheet of filo pastry, leaving any excess pastry hanging over the edges. Brush the sheet with melted butter, then place another sheet of filo over it and brush with melted butter. Continue doing this until you have used up all the sheets.

Pour the cooled custard inside, then arrange the berries all over, pressing them down gently into the custard.

Bake in the oven for 30–35 minutes until the pastry becomes a golden brown and the custard is slightly golden.

Remove from the oven, leave to cool, then serve.

This lovely lemon tart has the added kick of limoncello liqueur, making it an ideal dessert when having guests over for dinner. The grated dark chocolate at the end combines really well with the lemon—in fact, where I come from on the Amalfi Coast, it is quite common to find limoncello-filled chocolates, which are delicious! Serve with a glass of cold limoncello for the perfect after-dinner treat.

CROSTATA ALLA CREMA DI LIMONCELLO CON CIOCCOLATO

Creamy Limoncello Tart with Grated Chocolate

Serves 8

FOR THE PASTRY:
2 cups/9oz/250g all-
    purpose flour, sifted,
    plus extra for dusting
pinch of salt
9 tbsp/4½oz/125g cold
    unsalted butter, plus
    extra for greasing
¾ cup/2¾oz/75g sifted
    confectioner's sugar, plus
    extra for sprinkling
grated zest of 1 lemon
2 egg yolks, slightly beaten
FOR THE FILLING:
1 quantity of Thick
    Homemade Custard
    (see p.160)
3 tbsp limoncello liqueur
grated zest of 1 large lemon
dark chocolate (at least
    70% cocoa solids),
    for grating

First, make the pastry. Mix the flour and salt in a large bowl, add the butter, and rub it in until it resembles breadcrumbs. Stir in the confectioner's sugar and lemon zest, then add the egg yolks and mix well to form a smooth dough. Form into a ball, wrap in plastic wrap, and leave to chill for at least 30 minutes.

Preheat the oven to 400°F/200°C. Grease an 8½in/22cm tart pan with some melted butter, then dust with flour.

Make the filling. Make the custard according to the recipe on p.160. When you remove the custard from the heat, stir in the limoncello and lemon zest, then leave to cool.

On a lightly floured work surface, roll the pastry out to a thickness of about ¼in/5mm and use to line the prepared tart pan. Blind bake for about 20–25 minutes (the first 5 minutes with weights, then without, see p.159). Remove from the oven and allow the pastry to cool. Carefully remove the cooled pastry from the pan and place on a flat plate or board.

Fill the pastry with the limoncello custard, then grate over the chocolate and serve immediately or chill until required. Serve at room temperature.

These traditional Sardinian Easter pastries, also known as *formagelle* or *casadinas*, depending on region, are filled with ricotta or other local cheese. They are normally made with a pastry of flour, lard, and water, however, I prefer them with a rich shortcrust pastry like this one. The pastry can be a little crumbly while you're making it, so work quickly—if you find it too crumbly, place it in the refrigerator for a few minutes to harden before continuing. If you prefer, you can mold the pastries in small tartlet pans, but formed by hand, they resemble little handmade baskets and are really very pretty and unusual. Delicate and not so sweet, they are perfect if you don't have a sweet tooth.

PERDULAS
Sardinian Ricotta Tartlets

Makes 8–10 tartlets

FOR THE PASTRY:
2 cups/9oz/250g all-purpose flour, sifted
10 tbsp/5oz/140g cold unsalted butter, cut into
   small pieces
1 large egg yolk, mixed with 2 tbsp ice-cold water
FOR THE FILLING:
1 cup/9oz/250g ricotta
pinch of salt
1 large egg
3 tbsp sugar
2 tsp semolina
grated zest of ½ lemon
grated zest of ½ orange
pinch of saffron powder

First, make the pastry. Place the flour in a bowl, add the butter, and rub it in until it resembles breadcrumbs. Add the egg yolk mixture, quickly mixing it in with your hands to form a dough, and adding a little more ice-cold water, if necessary. Form the pastry into a ball or flatten into a disc, wrap in plastic, and leave to chill for about 30 minutes.

Preheat the oven to 425°F/220°C. Line a large baking tray with parchment paper (or use greased individual tartlet pans).

Meanwhile, make the filling. Place the ricotta in a bowl and mash it lightly with a fork. Stir in a pinch of salt, the egg, sugar, semolina, zests, and saffron powder until everything is well incorporated. Cover and chill until required.

On a lightly floured work surface, roll out the pastry to a thickness of about ½in/1cm. Cut out circles using a 4¼in/11cm pastry cutter. Place one circle in the palm of your hand, then place 2 tablespoons of the filling mixture in the center. With your other hand, pinch the sides all around so the filling does not escape and the tartlet resembles a little basket. Carefully place on the prepared baking tray and bake in the oven for 20 minutes until well risen and golden brown.

Remove from the oven, leave to cool, and enjoy!

For the Neapolitans, these pies are made during Easter, symbolizing rebirth and fertility—a myth that dates back to pagan times, when the Neapolitans offered the fruits of the land to the mermaid *Partenope*—eggs for fertility, wheat from the earth, and ricotta from the shepherds. The recipe has evolved over the years and is now made not only at home but in pastry shops all over the region of Campania during Easter. At this time of year, I usually make a selection of larger pies and small ones like these for family and friends to enjoy. The *grana cotta* (pre-cooked wheat) can be found in good Italian delis.

PASTIERINE DI GRANO
Mini Wheat and Ricotta Pies

Makes 6

FOR THE PASTRY:
scant 2½ cups/10½oz/300g all-purpose flour,
    plus extra for flouring
1 stick/4oz/115g cold unsalted butter,
    cut into pieces, plus extra for greasing
scant ⅔ cup/4oz/120g superfine sugar
grated zest of 1 orange
2 large egg yolks
egg wash (see p.13)

FOR THE FILLING:
10½oz/300g jar or can of *grana cotta*, pre-cooked
    wheat (sold in Italian delis or online)
½ cup/120ml whole milk
1 tbsp/½oz/15g butter
1 tsp ground cinnamon
scant 1¼ cups/10½oz/300g ricotta
seeds of ½ vanilla bean
1 cup/7oz/200g sugar
grated zest of 1 orange
1 tbsp orange blossom water
2 eggs
1 egg yolk

FOR THE CREAM:
⅔ cup/150ml whole milk
¼ vanilla bean, split in half lengthways
2 egg yolks
5 tbsp/2¼oz/60g sugar
1 tbsp cornstarch

FOR THE TOP:
confectioner's sugar, for dusting

First, make the pastry. Sift the flour into a large bowl, add the butter, and rub it in until it resembles breadcrumbs. Stir in the sugar and orange zest, then add the egg yolks and mix to form a smooth pastry. You may need to add a little cold water, but do this very gradually—just a couple of drops at a time until the dough forms. Form into a ball and wrap in plastic wrap. Leave to chill for at least 30 minutes.

Meanwhile, make the filling. Place the wheat, milk, butter, and cinnamon in a small saucepan and gently bring to a boil, stirring until the milk has been absorbed. Remove from the heat and set aside to cool.

Make the cream. Place the milk in a saucepan with the vanilla bean and bring almost to boiling point, then remove from the heat. Meanwhile, whisk the egg yolks and sugar together in a heatproof bowl until light and creamy. Stir in the cornstarch and whisk until smooth. Gradually pour in the hot milk, whisking all the time to avoid lumps forming. When everything is well incorporated, pour back into the pan and return to medium heat, stirring constantly until it begins to bubble. Remove and leave to cool.

Whisk the ricotta, vanilla seeds, sugar, orange zest, and orange blossom water into the cooled wheat mixture. Gradually add the eggs and yolk, then stir in the cream and mix well together. Set aside.

Preheat the oven to 350°F/180°C. Grease 6 loose-bottomed tartlet pans, about 4½in/12cm in diameter, with melted butter and dust with flour.

On a lightly floured work surface, roll the dough out to a thickness of about ¼in/5mm and use to line the prepared tartlet pans. Lightly prick the bottoms with a fork, then fill each with the creamy mixture. Gather up the remaining bits of pastry, roll out, cut out thin strips, and arrange them so they criss-cross over the filling. Brush with a little egg wash. Place on a large flat baking tray and bake in the oven for 45 minutes until golden brown.

Remove from the oven, leave to cool, then dust with confectioner's sugar.

This nutritious pumpkin tart is influenced by the classic American pumpkin pie, with the Italian addition of creamy mascarpone. Pumpkin is widely used in Italy, especially for savory dishes like pasta and risotto, and it is added to stews and used to fill ravioli. Pumpkin is slightly sweet so it is ideal to use in desserts; I remember once during the fall, when I had an abundance of pumpkins, making a pumpkin crumble that went down really well at my restaurant. I think with the American influence of Halloween in Italy these days, sweet pumpkin dishes such as these are becoming increasingly popular.

CROSTATA DI ZUCCA
Pumpkin Tart

Serves 6

FOR THE PASTRY:
2 cups/9oz/250g all-
  purpose flour, sifted, plus
  extra for dusting
pinch of salt
9 tbsp/4½oz/125g cold
  unsalted butter, cut into
  small pieces, plus extra
  for greasing
½ cup/3½oz/100g sugar
2 egg yolks, lightly beaten
FOR THE FILLING:
1lb/480g pumpkin or
  butternut squash, peeled,
  seeds removed (to make
  14oz/400g)
generous ¾ cup/6¼oz/
  180g mascarpone cheese
2 tbsp soft brown sugar
pinch of ground cinnamon
pinch of grated nutmeg
1 tbsp Marsala or other
  sweet wine

To make the pastry, mix the flour and salt together in a large bowl, add the butter, and rub it into the flour until it resembles breadcrumbs. Stir in the sugar, then add the egg yolks and mix well to form a dough. Wrap in plastic wrap and leave to chill for about 30 minutes.

Preheat the oven to 400°F/200°C.

Cut the pumpkin into thin slices, place on a baking tray, and bake in the oven for about 30 minutes until softened. Remove, place in a bowl, and mash to a soft pulp. Leave to cool, then stir in the mascarpone, sugar, cinnamon, nutmeg, and Marsala until everything is well incorporated.

Reduce the oven temperature to 325°F/160°C. Grease a 9½in/24cm round tart pan with a little melted butter, then dust with flour.

On a lightly floured work surface, roll the dough out to a thickness of ¼in/5mm and use to line the prepared tart pan. Trim off the excess pastry and set aside. Fill the pastry with the pumpkin mixture. Reroll the excess pastry, cut it into thin strips, and place in a lattice pattern over the top of the filling. Bake in the oven for 30 minutes until the pastry is golden.

Remove from the oven and cool before slicing and serving.

This traditional Austrian dessert is also common in the northern Italian regions of Trentino-Alto Adige and Veneto, whose borders neighbor Austria. It is often made with store-bought filo pastry, but here I have given you the typical pastry made in Alto Adige. Simple to make, the trick is to get it as thin as you can when rolling it out. The addition of breadcrumbs helps to bind the filling and soak up the juices during baking. It can be enjoyed warm as a dessert with some custard or ice cream, and is delicious eaten cold with afternoon tea.

STRUDEL DI MELE
Apple Strudel

Serves 6–8

FOR THE PASTRY:
1 cup/4½oz/125g all-purpose flour, sifted, plus extra for dusting
pinch of salt
1 egg
1 tbsp extra virgin olive oil
3 tbsp lukewarm water
FOR THE FILLING:
7 tbsp/3½oz/100g unsalted butter
about ¼ cup/1½oz/40g mixed dried fruit, chopped if large, soaked in enough lukewarm water to cover
¾ cup/2¾oz/75g dried breadcrumbs
1lb 5oz/600g Golden Delicious apples, peeled, cored, and thinly sliced
1 tsp ground cinnamon
grated zest of 1 lemon
¼ cup/1¾oz/50g sugar
¼ cup/1¼oz/35g roughly chopped walnuts
confectioner's sugar, for sprinkling

To make the pastry, place the flour and salt in a large bowl, add the egg, olive oil, and lukewarm water, and mix into a fairly sticky dough. Place on a lightly floured work surface and knead gently for a minute or so, adding a little more flour if required, until well incorporated. Form into a ball. Lightly grease a bowl, place the dough into it, cover with plastic wrap, and leave in a cool place for 30 minutes.

Preheat the oven to 400°F/200°C. Line a flat baking tray with parchment paper.

For the filling, melt half of the butter in a small pan, add the breadcrumbs, and fry, stirring over medium heat until toasted and golden brown. Be careful not to burn them! Remove from the heat and leave to cool.

Drain the mixed fruit well and combine with the apples, cinnamon, zest, and sugar. Stir in the cooled breadcrumbs.

Place a clean cloth or dish towel on your work surface and lightly dust with flour. Place the pastry on top and roll out to a rectangular shape, about 16 x 14in/40 x 35cm, or as thin as you can get it. If the pastry is too sticky, dust with a little flour.

Melt the remaining butter and brush some of it over the pastry, leaving a border of about ¾in/2cm. Arrange the apple mixture over this and top with the chopped walnuts. With the help of the cloth, roll into a long sausage shape, sealing the ends to stop the filling from escaping, and place on the prepared tray. Brush the top with more melted butter and bake in the oven for 30 minutes until slightly golden.

Remove from the oven and leave to cool slightly before sprinkling with confectioner's sugar and slicing.

BISCOTTI Cookies

Biscotti, as the name suggests, means double-baked, since this is how they were traditionally made. In fact, early Italian cookies were slices of bread that were re-baked in the oven to make them crispy and last longer. Known as *pan biscotto,* they were dunked in water or milk to soften for ease of eating. These types of cookie were made for sailors to consume during long voyages or were given to soldiers away at war.

In Medieval times, the art of cookie making was perfected in convents and monasteries and this has shaped the way they are made in Italy today. In the village of Erice in Sicily, a young girl named Maria Grammatico entered the convent in the 1940s and was taught how to bake by the nuns; she perfected this skill and eventually left the convent to open her own shop in the village—the shop is still there and famous for its almond cookies, attracting locals and tourists from far and wide.

From about the mid-1800s, cookies were produced commercially, and it was during this era that Davide Lazzaroni set up his famous cookie empire, selling cookies in beautifully decorated tin boxes. I remember seeing boxes like this at home in Italy, and when the cookies were all eaten, the box would always remain and be used for storing other cookies or for other household purposes. *Lazzaroni* is still a famous name among Italian cookie producers, and the cookies are exported all over the world. Probably the best known outside of Italy are the *Amaretti di Saronno* sold in the traditional red boxes.

Of course, the cookies we love and enjoy today evolved over the ages with the introduction of new and exciting ingredients and methods of production. Chocolate-covered cookies or cookies sandwiched together with various fillings appeared in the last 50 years or so.

As with all Italian food, cookies, too, vary from region to region. Probably one of the most renowned is the Tuscan *cantuccini*—known outside of Italy as *biscotti*— and these are still baked twice to achieve a crispy texture. The soft, sponge-like *savoiardi* from Piemonte have age-old roots and are said to have originally been made for royalty. In the Naples area, rich and spicy honey *mostaccioli* and *rococo* cookies are popular. And in Sicily, almond-based cookies, often sold in different colors and decorated with candied fruit, are a joy to look at and eat.

These simple cookies are just the best! They are so good that once you start to eat one, you can't stop; the dough is so delicate that the cookies just melt in your mouth. I like to add vanilla, but you can add other flavorings if you prefer, such as lemon or orange zest. I use a round cutter, but you can make them into lots of different and interesting shapes—my girls love to experiment! They are also a great basis for my Jam or Nutella cookies, see opposite and p.184.

BASIC COOKIES

Makes 22 cookies

scant 1¼ cups/5½oz/150g all-purpose flour,
    plus extra for flouring
7 tbsp/3½oz/100g cold unsalted butter, cut into
    small chunks
⅔ cup/2½oz/70g sifted confectioner's sugar
seeds of ½ vanilla bean
1 egg yolk

Sift the flour into a bowl, add the butter, and rub it in until it resembles breadcrumbs. Mix in the confectioner's sugar and vanilla seeds. Add the egg yolk and mix into a smooth dough, working quickly to avoid the dough getting warm. Form the dough into a ball, wrap in plastic wrap, and leave to chill for at least 30 minutes, or until required.

Preheat the oven to 375°F/190°C. Line a large flat baking tray with parchment paper.

On a lightly floured work surface, roll out the dough to a thickness of about ¼in/5mm. Using a 2in/5cm round cookie cutter (or any shape you like), cut out 22 rounds and arrange them on the prepared pan, leaving a little space for them to expand. Bake in the oven for about 10 minutes until lightly golden.

Remove from the oven, leave to cool, and enjoy! Store in an airtight container for up to a week.

These popular jam cookies can be found in bakeries and cake shops all over Italy and are made in various shapes and sizes. They are really simple to make at home and fun to make with the children, who will love them! If you can, use homemade or good-quality jam.

BISCOTTI CON LA MARMELLATA
Jam Cookies

Makes about 11 cookies

1 quantity of Basic Cookie dough (see opposite)
jam of your choice, such as strawberry, raspberry, or
   apricot, sieved
a little sugar, for sprinkling

Make the Basic Cookie dough according to the recipe opposite. Form the dough into a ball, wrap in plastic wrap, and leave to chill for at least 30 minutes.

Preheat the oven to 375°F/190°C. Line a flat baking tray with parchment paper.

On a lightly floured work surface, roll out the dough to a thickness of about ¼in/5mm and cut out about 22 circles using a 2in/5cm round pastry cutter. Using a tiny cookie cutter or the round end of a pastry bag tip, make a small hole in the center of half of the circles. On the circles without holes, place a dollop of jam. Sandwich with the remaining circles (the ones with the hole). The jam should be visible, but be careful not to press too hard or it will escape during cooking.

Arrange the cookies on the prepared pan, leaving some room for them to expand, sprinkle with sugar, and bake in the oven for about 15 minutes until golden.

Remove from the oven and leave to cool. Store in an airtight container for up to a week.

Quick and simple to make, these cookies are a joy to eat! The dough is delicate and just like Basic Cookies (see p.182) with the addition of orange zest. Once cooked, they are sandwiched together with Nutella spread. I am sure the kids will love to help out with these. They will keep for a week if stored properly, but I doubt they will last that long!

BISCOTTI ALLA NUTELLA
Nutella Cookies

Makes 11 cookies

scant 1¼ cups/5½oz/150g all-purpose flour
7 tbsp/3½oz/100g cold unsalted butter, cut into
    small chunks
⅔ cup/2½oz/70g sifted confectioner's sugar,
    plus extra for sprinkling
grated zest of ½ orange
seeds of ½ vanilla bean
1 egg yolk
½ small jar (about 3½oz/100g) of Nutella

Sift the flour into a bowl, add the butter, and rub it in until it resembles breadcrumbs. Mix in the confectioner's sugar, orange zest, and vanilla seeds. Add the egg yolk and work into a smooth dough, working quickly to avoid the dough getting warm. Form the dough into a ball, wrap in plastic wrap, and leave to chill for at least 30 minutes, or until required.

Preheat the oven to 375°F/190°C. Line 2 flat baking trays with parchment paper.

On a lightly floured work surface, roll out the dough to a thickness of about ¼in/5mm. Using a 2in/5cm round cookie cutter, cut out 22 circles and place them on the prepared pans, leaving a little room for them to expand. Bake in the oven for about 10 minutes until golden.

Remove from the oven, leave to cool, then sandwich together with some Nutella. Arrange on a plate and sprinkle with a little confectioner's sugar. Store in an airtight container for up to a week.

These cookies come from *Castellamare*, the hometown of my mother. They were always a treat when we went to visit my grandparents or when they came to visit us. We would eat them dipped in our morning milk or at teatime with hot chocolate. I really wanted to recreate them for this book, since they evoke happy childhood memories and they are not the kind of cookie you can easily find outside of this particular town. They are made from a leavened dough, traditionally made using the local carbonated spring water. For the purposes of recreating the recipe at home, I used Badoit water, which is only slightly sparkling.

BISCOTTI DI CASTELLAMARE
Childhood Cookies

Makes about 16 cookies

FOR THE STARTER DOUGH:
just under ½oz/12g fresh yeast (or use approximately 2 heaped tsp/¼oz/6g active-dry yeast, see p.13)
3 tbsp lukewarm water
1¼ cups/5½oz/150g white bread flour
FOR THE COOKIES:
2 cups/9oz/250g white bread flour
scant ½ cup/3¼oz/90g sugar
3 tbsp/1½oz/40g unsalted butter, softened at room temperature
grated zest of ½ lemon
½ cup/120ml naturally carbonated water
FOR DUSTING:
about 2 tsp confectioner's sugar, sifted
½ tsp ground cinnamon

First make the starter dough. Dissolve the yeast in the lukewarm water, add the flour, and mix well to form a dough. Knead into a ball, cover with plastic, and leave to rest in a warm place for 1 hour.

Preheat the oven to 375°F/190°C. Line a flat baking tray with parchment paper.

Place the starter dough on your work surface, open it out a little, and knead in the rest of the cookie ingredients until everything is well incorporated and a smooth dough has formed.

Roll pieces of the dough into cigar-type shapes about 6in/15cm long. Place on the prepared tray, leaving some room for them to expand, cover with a cloth, and rest at room temperature for 10 minutes.

Mix the confectioner's sugar and cinnamon together and sprinkle over the top of the cookies. Bake for about 25–30 minutes until golden.

Remove from the oven and leave to cool. These can be stored in an airtight container for up to a week.

Also known as *bussolai* or *buranelli*, these simple but tasty cookies originate from the lovely Venetian island of Burano, where traditionally they were made during Easter. They are now very popular around Venice all year round and can be found wrapped in cellophane and sold in bakeries or offered at the end of a meal in restaurants, along with a glass of sweet dessert wine. They are made into an "S" shape or can also be rings.

BISCOTTI VENEZIANI BURANELLI
Venetian Cookies

Makes about 22 cookies

2 cups/9oz/250g all-purpose flour
pinch of salt
5½ tbsp/2¾oz/75g unsalted butter,
    softened at room temperature
½ cup/3½oz/100g sugar
3 egg yolks, beaten
1 tsp vanilla extract
1 tbsp rum
grated zest of 1 lemon

Sift the flour and salt into a large bowl. Add the remaining ingredients and mix well to form a smooth dough. Wrap in plastic wrap and leave to chill for at least 30 minutes.

Meanwhile, preheat the oven to 350°F/180°C. Line 2 large flat baking trays with parchment paper.

Place the dough on a lightly floured work surface. Slice off a piece of dough and roll into a long thin sausage shape. Cut off 4½in/12cm lengths and form into "S" shapes. Continue doing this with the rest of the pastry. Place the cookies on the prepared trays and bake in the oven for about 15–20 minutes until golden.

Remove from the oven and leave to cool slightly. Store in an airtight container for up to a week.

Very simple to make, but make sure you use the best lemons you can get for ideal results—Amalfi lemons are best, but hard to find in the USA. If you prefer, you can omit the glaze and enjoy the cookies plain; you will still taste the lemony tang from the zest in the dough.

BISCOTTI AL LIMONE
Lemon Cookies

Makes about 22 cookies

scant 1¼ cups/5½oz/150g all-purpose flour,
   plus extra for flouring
7 tbsp/3½oz/100g cold unsalted butter,
   cut into small chunks
⅔ cup/2½oz/70g sifted confectioner's sugar
grated zest of 2 lemons
1 egg yolk
FOR THE LEMON GLAZE:
¾ cup/2¾oz/75g sifted confectioner's sugar
juice of ½ lemon
grated zest of 1 lemon

Sift the flour into a bowl, add the butter, and rub it in until it resembles breadcrumbs. Mix in the confectioner's sugar and lemon zest. Add the egg yolk and mix into a smooth dough, working quickly to avoid the dough getting warm. Form the dough into a ball, wrap in plastic, and chill for at least 30 minutes, or until required.

Preheat the oven to 375°F/190°C. Line a baking tray with parchment paper.

On a lightly floured work surface, roll out the dough to a thickness of about ¼in/5mm. Using a 2in/5cm round cookie cutter (or any shaped cutter you prefer), cut the dough into circles and place on the prepared pan. Bake in the oven for about 10 minutes until lightly golden.

Remove from the oven and leave to cool for 2 minutes on the pan, then transfer to a wire rack to cool completely.

To make the glaze, place the sifted confectioner's sugar in a bowl and gradually add enough lemon juice to make a smooth icing (you may need more or less juice). Stir in the zest, then drizzle the icing over the cookies. Leave to set for 20–30 minutes. These cookies can be stored in an airtight container for up to a week.

These typical Italian cookies date back to the early 1800s, when they were made during Easter in the shape of little baskets and children would put colored eggs inside. Over time, these popular cookies have evolved into a flower shape and are eaten at any time. They are made industrially to be sold in shops and supermarkets all over Italy and exported abroad. However, the homemade version is so much tastier. The combination of potato flour and the unusual addition of hard-boiled egg yolks give these cookies their characteristic crumbly melt-in-your-mouth texture. Once you start eating, you will not be able to stop!

CANESTRELLI
Flower-Shaped Cookies

Makes about 50 cookies

4 eggs
1⅔ cups/7oz/200g all-purpose flour, sifted,
    plus extra for flouring
scant 1 cup/5½oz/150g potato flour
1¾ sticks/7oz/200g cold unsalted butter,
    cut into pieces
1 cup/3½oz/100g sifted confectioner's sugar,
    plus extra for dusting
2 tsp vanilla extract
grated zest of 1 lemon

Cook the eggs until hard-boiled, leave to cool, then remove the shell and discard the whites (or save for another use). Crumble up the yolks and set aside.

Combine the flours in a large bowl, add the butter, and rub it in until it resembles breadcrumbs. Stir in the confectioner's sugar, vanilla, and zest, and push the egg yolks through a sieve into the mixture. Mix well to form a very smooth dough, wrap in plastic, and leave to chill for 1 hour.

Preheat the oven to 325°F/160°C. Line a baking tray with parchment paper.

On a floured work surface, roll out the dough to a thickness of ½in/1cm. Cut out flower shapes using a 2in/5cm flower-shaped cookie cutter, then cut out a small circle from the center of each one using a tiny round cookie cutter or the bottom of pastry bag tip. Place on the prepared baking tray and bake for 17–20 minutes until just becoming golden.

Remove from the oven, leave to cool, then sprinkle with confectioner's sugar. These can be stored in an airtight container for 2 weeks.

These Tuscan specialty cookies originate from the city of Siena and are traditionally given as gifts at Christmas. However, there is no reason why you can't enjoy these slightly chewy almond-based treats at any time. They date back from ancient times, when a noble knight, Ricciardetto della Gheradesca, returned home from the Crusades. To celebrate his safe return, these cookies were created using almonds from the Middle East, with their pointed shape resembling Turkish slippers. The original recipe is made with ground bitter almonds; however, using regular ground almonds with a few drops of almond extract is equally delicious. Since no flour is used, they are ideal for anyone on a gluten-free diet. Nowadays, they are commercially made and widely available in good pastry shops all over Italy; however, they are so simple to make and you can add less sugar to suit your taste. You will need to start this recipe the night before.

RICCIARELLI
Tuscan Almond Cookies (Gluten-Free)

Makes about 15 cookies

2⅔ cups/9oz/250g ground almonds
1½ cups/6¼oz/180g confectioner's sugar, sifted,
    plus extra for dusting
1 tsp almond or vanilla extract
whites of 2 small eggs

Combine the ground almonds and confectioner's sugar in a large bowl, then add the vanilla extract.

In another bowl, whisk the egg whites until stiff. Fold the egg whites into the ground almond mixture until a sticky dough has formed. Don't worry if it feels a little too sticky. Wrap the dough in plastic wrap and leave to chill overnight or for at least 12 hours.

Preheat the oven to 325°F/160°C. Line a baking tray with parchment paper.

Lightly dust your work surface with some confectioner's sugar and, using your hands, roll the dough into a long thick sausage. Cut out chunks weighing about 1oz/25g each, then flatten and form into diamond shapes, roughly ½in/1cm thick and 4in/10cm in length. Dust all over with lots of confectioner's sugar, then place on the prepared baking tray.

Bake the cookies in the oven for 12 minutes. Do not allow them to color; they are supposed to be white. Remove from the oven, leave to cool for a few minutes on the baking tray, then transfer to a wire rack to cool completely. Enjoy, or store in an airtight container for up to a week.

The classic Tuscan *cantucci* cookies (widely known as biscotti) have evolved quite a lot over the last few years. They were originally made with almonds and used to dip into the sweet wine Vin Santo for special occasions, but now you can add all kinds of ingredients and flavors. I especially like these, which I enjoy with a mid-morning cappuccino.

CANTUCCINI CON PISTACCHIO E CIOCCOLATO BIANCO
Cantuccini with Pistachio and White Chocolate

Makes about 24

generous 1 cup/5½oz/150g shelled pistachios
scant 2½ cups/10½oz/300g all-purpose flour
½ tsp baking powder
pinch of salt
2 eggs
scant ½ cup/3oz/80g sugar
¼ cup/60ml heavy cream
3½oz/100g white chocolate, roughly chopped

Preheat the oven to 425°F/220°C.

Place the pistachios on a baking tray and roast in the oven for 10 minutes. Remove and set aside.

Turn the oven down to 375°F/190°C. Line a large flat baking tray with parchment paper.

Sift the flour, baking powder, and salt together.

Whisk the eggs and sugar together in a large bowl until light and creamy. Stir in the cream, then fold in the flour mixture. Add the chocolate and roasted pistachios and mix well to form a dough.

Divide the dough in half and roll each half into a sausage shape 14in/35cm long and 2in/5cm wide. Place on the prepared baking tray and bake in the oven for 15 minutes.

Remove from the oven and cut each sausage diagonally into slices of about ¾in/2cm using a sharp knife. Lay them flat on the baking tray and return to the oven for a further 10 minutes, or until crunchy. Remove from the oven, leave to cool, and serve, or store in an airtight container for up to a week.

These traditional Neapolitan cookies have been around for centuries and are normally prepared at Christmastime. The name comes from *mosto* (must), since this was traditionally used to sweeten them. They are made in the classical diamond shape and sold in confectionery shops all over the region. For me, they symbolize Christmas and I always make sure I have some to remind me of home. I have given you a large quantity because it is traditional in Italy to make lots and give them away to family and friends as gifts. You don't have to make the full quantity but if you do, you can always freeze the dough. To give them more of a festive twist, I have made them into star shapes.

MOSTACCIOLI
Christmas Cookies

Makes about 60 cookies

8 cups/2lb 4oz/1kg all-purpose flour, sifted
2 tsp baking powder, sifted
3 cups/1lb 5oz/600g sugar
2½ tbsp pumpkin pie spice
3¼ cups/10½oz/300g ground almonds
generous ½ cup/1¾oz/50g unsweetened cocoa powder, sifted
generous ¾ cup/200ml honey
⅔ cup/7oz/200g apricot jam
¾ cup/180ml sweet wine (like Marsala or Vin Santo)
¾ cup/180ml tepid water
FOR THE TOPPING:
about 2lb 12oz/1.2kg dark chocolate (at least 70% cocoa solids), broken into pieces
edible silver beads, sprinkles, or crushed nuts (optional)

Combine all of the cookie ingredients together in a large bowl or on a clean work surface and mix into a smooth dough. Form into a ball, wrap in plastic, and leave to chill for 24 hours.

Preheat the oven to 350°F/180°C. Line large flat baking trays with parchment paper.

On a lightly floured work surface, roll out the dough to a thickness of ½in/1cm and cut out star shapes with a 4in/10cm star-shaped cutter. Brush off any excess flour with a little water. Place on the prepared baking trays and bake in the oven for 20 minutes.

Remove from the oven and leave to cool for a few minutes on the tray, then transfer to a wire rack to cool completely.

For the topping, melt the chocolate in a heatproof bowl suspended over a pan of gently simmering water, making sure the base of the bowl doesn't touch the water. Dip the cookies into the melted chocolate to cover them completely, sprinkle with your chosen topping, and leave to set overnight on parchment paper. These can be stored in an airtight container for up to a month.

Almond-based cakes and cookies are typical of Sicily, where almonds grow in abundance. Traditionally these cookies are made in different colors for special occasions, such as weddings and christenings. Simple and quick to make, they do look very pretty, and you can color and decorate as you like. If you prefer to keep them plain, they are just as delicious. They are also perfect for anyone with a gluten intolerance!

PASTICCINI DI MANDORLA SICILIANI COLORATI
Sicilian Colored Almond Cookies

Makes about 24

2 egg whites
scant 1 cup/9oz/250g
    ground almonds
generous 1 cup/7¾oz/220g
    sugar
2 tsp honey
4 drops of almond extract
grated zest of 1 orange
green and red food
    coloring (optional)
a little confectioner's sugar
    and granulated sugar, for
    sprinkling
candied cherries, angelica,
    and whole blanched
    almonds, to decorate

Preheat the oven to 350°F/180°C. Line a large baking tray with parchment paper.

Whisk the egg whites until nearly stiff, then set aside.

Combine the ground almonds and sugar in a large bowl, then add the honey, almond extract, and orange zest. Fold in the egg whites and mix gently until a smooth, sticky dough-like consistency has formed.

If coloring your cookies, divide the mixture into 3 portions. Add a few drops of red coloring to one piece and knead it in until it is a uniform color. Do the same with the green food coloring, and leave one piece its natural color.

Place one colored mixture into a pastry bag fitted with a large star-shaped tip and pipe out rosettes, about 2in/5cm in diameter, onto the prepared baking tray. Do the same with the next color and the one after. The mixture is quite stiff so a little patience is needed while piping, but the effort will be worth it!

Mix the confectioner's and granulated sugars together and sprinkle over the rosettes, then decorate with the cherries, angelica, and almonds. Bake in the oven for 7–10 minutes until just beginning to color.

Remove from the oven and leave to cool, during which time the cookies will harden slightly. They can be stored in an airtight container for up to a week.

These classic light sponge fingers are widely used in preparing Italian desserts such as *tiramisu* and *zuppa inglese*. However, they are also lovely eaten on their own with tea or dipped in a cappuccino. Being fat-free and easily digestible, *savoiardi* are a popular choice in Italy with young children, convalescents, and the elderly. Although industrially produced and found in most shops, they are very simple and quick to make at home and of course taste much nicer.

SAVOIARDI ALLA VANIGLIA
Vanilla Sponge Fingers

Makes about 20 cookies

⅓ cup/2½oz/70g superfine sugar
2 eggs, separated
generous ¼ cup/1¼oz/35g all-purpose flour, sifted
2 tsp potato flour, sifted
pinch of salt
seeds of 1 vanilla bean
2 tsp confectioner's sugar, sifted

Preheat the oven to 400°F/200°C. Line 2 large flat baking trays with parchment paper.

Place 2 tablespoons of the sugar and the egg yolks in a bowl and whisk until light and creamy. In another clean bowl, whisk another 2 tablespoons of the sugar with the egg whites until stiffened.

Combine the flours and salt together and then fold into the egg yolk mixture. Add the vanilla seeds, then fold in the stiffened egg whites until everything is well incorporated.

Place the mixture into a pastry bag fitted with a smooth tip and pipe 4in/10cm fingers onto the prepared baking tray, spacing them apart, since they expand while baking.

Mix the remaining tablespoon or so of sugar and the confectioner's sugar together and sprinkle all over the *savoiardi*. Bake for 10 minutes until golden. These can be stored in an airtight container for up to a week.

TORTE Cakes

Who can possibly resist a homemade cake?

Traditionally cakes were not as we know them today—often the only factor that put them in the cake category was a round shape. They tended to be more bread-like with perhaps the addition of honey as a sweetener. The ancient Romans added butter and eggs, and a more cake-like consistency and texture were evident, but still nothing like the cakes we know and love today.

As with all food, cakes, too, have evolved throughout the ages but the basic ingredients of flour, sugar, eggs, and butter are the norm in most cakes. Some cakes in Italy omit butter, and the eggs are often separated; the yolks are whisked with sugar and the whites whisked until stiff, flour is then folded in, and the three ingredients combined. This whisking method results in a light sponge cake known as *Pan di Spagna* and forms the basis of many celebration cakes, which are filled and decorated according to the occasion. These are popular in cake shops throughout Italy, as well as easy to make at home.

Olive oil is a popular addition to Italian cakes and has long been used by Italian housewives, resulting in a deliciously moist cake. Ricotta and plain yogurt are also popular and healthy additions.

As in most parts of the world, a cake usually symbolizes a celebration, from simple homemade sponge cakes for a child's birthday, to fancy wedding cakes.

Over the years, cakes have become more elaborate and even children's birthday cakes are often themed with a superhero, cartoon character, or sport. When I was a child, a plain homemade sponge cake dusted with confectioner's sugar was the norm. Nowadays, with an abundance of food colorings, sugar paste, and unusually shaped pans all readily available in cookware stores or online, we can get creative and make cakes to impress.

Cakes with fresh fruit added to them are popular in Italy and a homey apple or pear cake makes a nice teatime treat. When you hear Italians talking about plum cake (see p.213), this has nothing to do with the addition of plums. They mean a cake that is baked in a loaf pan and usually has a little dried fruit or chocolate chips added to it.

Despite all the advances in cake making, I still prefer a simple cake like a plain sponge or olive oil cake, and it doesn't have to be a birthday or anniversary to enjoy it. Homemade cakes are a pleasure at any time and, because they are so simple, good-quality ingredients are important in achieving the best results. Try to get good-quality flour, if possible, superfine sugar, good-quality butter, and organic free-range eggs. When I was a child, the color of cake was always a lovely yellow because the eggs were so fresh and good. Whenever I'm in the countryside, I always stock up on the freshest of farm eggs. There is nothing more delicious than a simple cake made with good ingredients.

TIPS FOR CAKE MAKING

• Use the best ingredients you can afford, especially butter and eggs; they will really enhance the flavor of your cake.

• Preheat the oven to the correct temperature.

• Use the correct size pan as specified in the recipes.

• Remember to line and grease your pans accordingly.

• If the recipe asks for separating the eggs, make sure you beat the yolks and sugar really well and for a good 5 minutes, even with an electric mixer, until they are light, creamy, and you can almost make patterns with the mixture. Wash your blades and whisk the whites until stiff in a clean, dry bowl.

• Make sure you have a long enough wooden skewer on hand for inserting into the cake to check if it is cooked.

• Always leave the cake to cool completely before decorating or dusting with confectioner's sugar.

Despite its name, this is the typical Italian sponge cake made for birthdays and celebrations, and it makes the basis of many desserts. After baking and left to cool until cold, the sponge is drizzled with a syrup of water and alcohol to moisten it; if making for kids, you can substitute the alcohol with freshly squeezed orange juice, though the alcohol content is so diluted it really will not harm. I tend to use Marsala, since it's easier to find, but you can use Strega or Maraschino. The typical filling is a vanilla-flavored custard cream (*crème patissiere*), and cocoa powder can be added for a chocolate flavor. For a special cake, three or four layers are made with alternating flavored custard fillings and the top is decorated with mixed fruit. If you prefer, you can sandwich the layers with whipped cream and/or jam. I often like to make a plain sponge cake without the syrup and filling, and enjoy a slice or two with my morning espresso for breakfast. If you want to do the same, just use half this quantity and bake in an 8in/20cm cake pan for about 20–25 minutes. For a delicious cake, use the best quality free-range organic eggs you can get. It is the traditional lengthy whisking of the eggs and sugar that gives air to the cake, making it rise, and therefore not needing any additional rising agents.

TORTA PAN DI SPAGNA
Italian Sponge Cake

Serves 8

FOR THE SPONGE CAKE:
scant 1 cup/6¼oz/180g superfine sugar
6 eggs
pinch of salt
1 tsp vanilla extract
scant 1½ cups/6¼oz/180g all-purpose flour, sifted
FOR THE FILLING:
generous 1 cup/250ml milk
½ vanilla bean
3 egg yolks
½ cup/3½oz/100g superfine sugar
scant ¼ cup/1oz/25g cornstarch
FOR THE SYRUP:
5 tbsp/70ml Marsala or other sweet wine
2 tbsp superfine sugar
3 slices orange rind
3 slices lemon rind
FOR THE TOP:
confectioner's sugar, for dusting (optional)   >>

Preheat the oven to 350°F/180°C. Lightly grease a 10½in/26cm round springform cake pan, then dust with flour.

Using an electric mixer, beat the sugar and eggs together for about 15 minutes until light and creamy and the mixture reaches the "ribbon" stage (when the whisk is lifted over the bowl, the mixture falls back, slowly forming a ribbon that will hold its shape for a few minutes). About halfway through, add the salt and vanilla. Using a spatula, gradually and gently fold in the flour until it is incorporated. Pour the mixture into the prepared pan and bake in the oven for 40 minutes until golden. Insert a wooden skewer to check if it is cooked through; if it comes out clean, the cake is done.

Remove from the oven, leave to cool for a few minutes, then turn out of the pan and leave to cool completely on a wire rack. Once cold, carefully slice into two layers. Set aside.

To make the filling, pour the milk into a small saucepan, add the vanilla bean, and heat until the milk reaches boiling point. Meanwhile, beat the egg yolks and sugar together in a large bowl until light and fluffy. Add the cornstarch and continue to whisk, then gradually pour the hot milk into the egg mixture, whisking constantly to prevent lumps forming. Once combined, pour the mixture back into the saucepan, place over medium heat, and stir with a wooden spoon. As soon as it begins to boil, remove from the heat, pour into a dish, and leave to cool.

To make the syrup, put 1¼ cups/300ml water in a small pan and add all of the syrup ingredients. Heat over medium heat, stirring all the time until the sugar has dissolved and the liquid has reduced by about one-third. Remove from the heat and leave to cool completely. Discard the rinds. Drizzle or brush the syrup over both layers of sponge cake.

Place one layer on a plate and spread with the custard filling, then sandwich together with the other layer of cake. Dust with the confectioner's sugar or decorate as you wish.

Fresh fruit is often added to cakes in Italy, and I remember my grandma making a similar cake to this one using apples. It's a tasty way to add more fruit to your diet, especially for children. Pear and dark chocolate go really well together and this makes a lovely cake to serve for afternoon tea.

TORTA DI PERE E CIOCCOLATO
Pear and Chocolate Cake

Serves 6–8

3 eggs
¾ cup/5½oz/150g superfine sugar
6 tbsp/3oz/85g unsalted butter, room temperature
scant 2½ cups/10½oz/300g self-rising flour, sifted
seeds of 1 vanilla bean
grated zest of 1 small unwaxed lemon
3 ripe pears, peeled, cored, and cut into chunks
2¾oz/75g dark chocolate (at least 70% cocoa
    solids), roughly broken into small chunks
FOR THE TOPPING:
½ cup/3½oz/100g superfine sugar
1 tbsp/½oz/15g unsalted butter
2 pears, sliced very thinly
a little sifted confectioner's sugar (optional)

Preheat oven to 400°F/200°C. Grease an 8in/20cm round springform cake pan and line with parchment paper.

Whisk the eggs and sugar together in a large bowl until light and fluffy. Add the softened butter and continue to whisk until it is well amalgamated. Fold in the flour, vanilla, lemon zest, pears, and chocolate. Pour the mixture into the prepared pan and bake in the oven for about 45 minutes. Insert a wooden skewer to check that it is cooked through; if it comes out clean, the cake is done. Remove from the oven and leave to cool. Loosen the cake and place on a serving plate.

To decorate, heat the sugar in a wide sauté pan over medium heat. Do not stir, just gently agitate the pan from time to time until the sugar starts to melt; this will take about 5 minutes. Continue to cook, gently stirring with a wooden spoon, for about 10 minutes, until a dark caramel forms. Stir the butter through and add the pear slices, turning to coat them in the caramel. Cook for 3–4 minutes until golden. Arrange on top of the cake. Decorate with sifted confectioner's sugar, if you like.

This delicious gluten-free cake originates from the town of Varese in the northern Lombardy region of Italy, where traditionally polenta was a main staple. Also known as *Dolce di Varese*, this cake was a popular Sunday treat and is now sold in pastry shops and cafés all over the region. Quick and easy to prepare, this almond-infused cake is lovely at teatime.

AMOR DI POLENTA!
Polenta and Almond Cake (Gluten-Free)

Serves 6

7 tbsp/3½oz/100g unsalted butter, softened
   at room temperature
½ cup/3½oz/100g sugar
2 eggs, lightly beaten
generous ¾ cup/3½oz/100g polenta cornmeal
½ cup/3oz/80g gluten-free all-purpose flour
1 tsp gluten-free baking powder
scant ¾ cup/2¾oz/75g ground almonds
1 tsp vanilla extract
1 tbsp Amaretto liqueur

Preheat the oven to 350°F/180°C and line a 7½ x 3¼in/19 x 8cm loaf pan with parchment paper.

Whisk the butter and sugar together in a large bowl until creamy. Gradually add the eggs, then fold in the flour, cornmeal, baking powder, and ground almonds. Add the vanilla and Amaretto, and fold in until it is incorporated.

Pour the mixture into the prepared pan and bake in the oven for 35 minutes, until golden brown. Insert a wooden skewer to check if it is cooked through; if it comes out clean, the cake is done.

Remove from the oven and leave to cool slightly, before turning out of the pan.

This is a twist on the traditional olive oil cake made for generations by Italian housewives. Years ago, olive oil was used instead of butter to make a plain and simple homemade cake. The addition of olive oil gives cake a much lighter texture, with all the added health benefits. I have taken the basic recipe and added some lemon and rosemary. Serving a raspberry coulis alongside the cake makes this a lovely dessert. You can, of course, replace the lemon and rosemary with grated orange zest, or chocolate, or any other flavor you prefer. The coulis can be made with strawberries or a selection of mixed berries.

TORTA ALL'OLIO CON LIMONE E ROSMARINO SERVITA CON SALSINA DI LAMPONI

Olive Oil Cake with Lemon and Rosemary Served with Raspberry Coulis

Serves 6

scant 1½ cups/6oz/170g self-rising flour, sifted
scant 1 cup/6oz/170g superfine sugar
grated zest of 2 large lemons
2 tsp finely chopped rosemary
scant 1 cup/215ml olive oil
5 eggs, lightly beaten
a little confectioner's sugar, sifted
FOR THE RASPBERRY COULIS (OPTIONAL):
1⅔ cups/7oz/200g raspberries
¼ cup/1¾oz/50g superfine sugar
juice of 1 blood orange

Preheat the oven to 325°F/160°C and line an 8in/20cm round springform cake pan with parchment paper.

Mix the flour, sugar, lemon zest, and rosemary together in a large bowl. Add the olive oil and eggs, and whisk until it is all well incorporated. Pour the mixture into the prepared cake pan and bake on the bottom part of the oven for 55–60 minutes. Insert a wooden skewer to check if it is cooked through; if it comes out clean, the cake is done.

Remove from the oven, cool slightly, then tip the cake out of the pan and leave to cool completely on a wire rack, before dusting with confectioner's sugar.

To make the coulis, place all the ingredients in a small pan, setting aside a few of the raspberries. Simmer over medium heat for about 7 minutes, or until the sauce begins to thicken. Remove from the heat, leave to cool slightly, stir in the whole raspberries, and serve with the cake.

In Italy, plum cake does not mean the inclusion of plums in a cake! It refers to a cake such as this one, cooked in a loaf pan and usually containing dried fruit. However, on a recent visit to my hometown, my niece made this lovely chocolate chip cake and referred to it as plum cake as well. A similar cake was served at breakfast at the hotel we were staying at, and Liz and my daughters couldn't get enough of it! So I decided it was only right to include this cake in this book and dedicate it to Anna, my niece. Made with ricotta and no butter, it is healthy and light and delicious at teatime or for breakfast.

PLUM CAKE DI ANNA
Chocolate Chip and Ricotta Loaf Cake

Serves 6–8

1 cup/9oz/250g ricotta
1¼ cups/9oz/250g superfine sugar
4 eggs, separated
seeds of 1 vanilla bean
2 cups/9oz/250g self-rising flour, sifted
pinch of salt
½ cup/3oz/80g dark chocolate chips

Preheat the oven to 350°F/180°C and line a 9½ x 5in/24 x 13cm loaf pan with parchment paper.

Whisk the ricotta and sugar together in a large bowl, then add the egg yolks and continue to whisk until light and creamy. Stir in the vanilla seeds, then fold in the flour and salt. Add the chocolate chips.

In a separate bowl, whisk the egg whites until stiff, then fold them into the cake mixture until well incorporated. Pour the mixture into the prepared pan and bake in the oven for about 50–60 minutes. Insert a wooden skewer to check if it is cooked through; if it comes out clean, the cake is done. If you notice the cake browning too much on the top before it is ready, cover the top with foil and continue baking.

Remove from the oven, leave to cool, then tip the cake out of the pan and serve.

This typical *Ciambella* has all the flavors of the rustic, homemade Italian cakes traditionally baked in a ring pan. It is made with olive oil instead of butter and the addition of yogurt makes it a very light and delicate cake. Be careful when removing it from the pan—it is so soft and light, it can easily break. Whenever I make this, it reminds me of the cakes my aunts and older sisters would make when I was a little boy. So simple, it is a perfect cake for afternoon tea.

CIAMBELLA ALLO YOGURT E ARANCIA
Yogurt and Orange Ring Cake

Serves 10

1½ cups/10½oz/300g superfine sugar
3 large eggs
juice of 1 orange
grated zest of 1 orange
generous 1 cup/250ml olive oil
scant ½ cup/3½oz/100g good-quality plain yogurt
scant 2½ cups/10½oz/300g self-rising flour, sifted
1 tsp baking powder, sifted
FOR THE TOPPING:
scant ½ cup/3½oz/100g good-quality plain yogurt
seeds of 1 vanilla bean
grated zest and juice of 1 orange
1 tbsp sifted confectioner's sugar
orange peel, to decorate

Preheat the oven to 400°F/200°C. Grease a 10½in/26cm ring or bundt pan and dust with flour.

Whisk the sugar and eggs together in a large bowl until creamy and the mixture turns a pale color. Add the orange juice and zest, olive oil, and yogurt and continue to whisk. Fold in the flour and baking powder until it is all well incorporated. Pour the mixture into the prepared pan and bake for 40–45 minutes until well risen and golden. Insert a wooden skewer to check if it is cooked through; if it comes out clean, the cake is done.

Remove from the oven, leave to cool completely, then turn the cake out of the pan.

To make the topping, combine the yogurt, vanilla, orange juice and zest, and confectioner's sugar. Pour over the cake and decorate with orange peel.

I love marble cake with a mix of vanilla and chocolate. To give it a bit of an Italian twist, I have added some espresso coffee and instead of the traditional ring pan, I have made it into a loaf. Light and delicate, it makes a perfect accompaniment to your mid-morning cup of espresso.

DOLCE MARMORIZZATO ALL'ESPRESSO
Marbled Espresso Loaf Cake

Serves 6

1 strong espresso (about ¼ cup/60ml)
¼ cup/60ml lukewarm milk
seeds of ½ vanilla bean or 1 tsp vanilla extract
15 tbsp/7½ oz/210g unsalted butter, softened at
    room temperature, plus more for greasing
1⅛ cups/8oz/225g superfine sugar
4 eggs, separated
scant 2 cups/8oz/240g self-rising flour, sifted
5 tbsp/1oz/25g unsweetened cocoa powder, sifted
confectioner's sugar, for sprinkling

Preheat the oven to 350°F/180°C. Grease a 8 x 4in/20 x 10cm loaf pan and line with parchment paper.

In a small bowl, combine the espresso with 2 tablespoons of the milk and the vanilla. Set aside.

Beat the butter and half of the sugar together in a large bowl until light and fluffy. In a separate bowl, beat the egg yolks and remaining sugar until creamy. Combine both mixtures together, then fold in the flour. Pour half of the mixture into another bowl. In one bowl, add the espresso mixture. In the other bowl, stir in the cocoa powder and remaining milk. In a separate clean bowl, whisk the egg whites until stiff, then divide between the mixtures, folding in well.

Place alternate dollops of the mixtures in the prepared pan and level the surface. Bake for 1 hour, or until well risen. Insert a wooden skewer to check if it is cooked through; if it comes out clean, the cake is done.

Remove from the oven, leave to cool, then transfer to a plate. Sift confectioner's sugar over the top, and serve in slices.

This traditional gluten-free chestnut specialty is very common during the fall in the regions of Emilia Romagna, Liguria, and Tuscany, where chestnuts are abundant and said to be the best in Italy. It has age-old roots, since chestnuts were once food of the poor—they were ground into flour and made into all kinds of dishes, including a cake-type dish like this one with the addition of water and rosemary, and as a treat some dried fruit would be added. Over time, as with all poor-man's dishes, this has become a sought-after delicacy, and it is now enriched with milk and pine nuts (I like to add a little dark chocolate too). Unless you want to grind your own chestnuts, the flour is available from good delis.

CASTAGNACCIO
Chestnut Squares

Makes 8 squares

2 tbsp raisins
Marsala or sweet wine, for soaking
scant 1⅔ cups/7oz/200g chestnut flour
pinch of salt
3 tbsp sugar
scant 2 cups/450ml milk
2 tbsp extra virgin olive oil
2½ tbsp pine nuts
needles of 1 rosemary sprig
1½oz/40g dark chocolate shavings (at least 70% cocoa solids)

Preheat the oven to 400°F/200°C and grease an 8 x 12in/20 x 30cm brownie pan with extra virgin olive oil.

Soak the raisins in enough sweet wine to just cover.

Combine the flour, salt, and sugar in a large bowl. Gradually whisk in the milk, olive oil, and 1 tablespoon of the wine, whisking well to avoid lumps. Stir in the pine nuts, raisins, rosemary needles, and half of the chocolate shavings. Pour the mixture into the prepared pan, top with the remaining chocolate shavings, and bake in the oven for 30 minutes. Insert a wooden skewer to check that it is cooked through; if it comes out clean, the cake is done.

Remove from the oven, leave to cool in the pan, then cut into squares.

INDEX

ACKNOWLEDGMENTS

Thanks to Liz Przybylski for researching and writing, to Adriana Contaldo for testing recipes and recreating them during the shoots, to Dan Jones for the gorgeous photos, to Emily Ezekiel for exquisite food styling, to Alexander Breeze for the prop styling, to Commissioning Editor Emily Preece-Morrison for being lovely and efficient, to Laura Russell and Miranda Harvey for the fantastic design, and finally, to Kathy Steer for correcting very efficiently and quickly!

First published in 2017 by

INTERLINK BOOKS
An imprint of Interlink Publishing Group, Inc.
46 Crosby Street, Northampton, MA 01060
www.interlinkbooks.com

Library of Congress Cataloging-in-Publication
Data available
ISBN 978-1-56656-017-7
10 9 8 7 6 5 4 3 2 1

Reproduction by Mission Productions Ltd.
Printed and bound in China

To request our 48-page, full-color catalog, please call us toll free at 1-800-238-LINK, visit our website at www.interlinkbooks.com, or send us an e-mail at: info@interlinkbooks.com.

When following the recipes, stick to one set of measurements (metric or imperial).